BSA

THE COMPLETE STORY

OTHER TITLES IN THE CROWOOD MOTOCLASSICS SERIES

AJS AND MATCHLESS Matthew Vale

BMW AIRHEAD TWINS Phil West

BMW GS Phil West

DOUGLAS Mick Walker

DUCATI DESMODUE Greg Pullen

FRANCIS-BARNETT Arthur Gent

GREEVES Colin Sparrow

HINCKLEY TRIUMPHS David Clarke

HONDA V4 Greg Pullen

MOTO GUZZI Greg Pullen

NORTON COMMANDO Matthew Vale

ROYAL ENFIELD Mick Walker

ROYAL ENFIELD BULLET Peter Henshaw

RUDGE-WHITWORTH Bryan Reynolds

TRIUMPH 650 AND 750 TWINS Matthew Vale

TRIUMPH PRE-UNIT TWINS Matthew Vale

VELOCETTE PRODUCTION MOTORCYCLES Mick Walker

VELOCETTE – THE RACING STORY Mick Walker

VINCENT David Wright

YAMAHA ROAD-RACING TWO-STROKES Colin MacKeller

BSA

THE COMPLETE STORY

GREG PULLEN

THE CROWOOD PRESS

First published in 2020 by
The Crowood Press Ltd
Ramsbury, Marlborough
Wiltshire SN8 2HR

enquiries@crowood.com

www.crowood.com

This impression 2021

British Library Cataloguing-in-Publication Data
A catalogue record for this book is available from the British Library.

ISBN 978 1 78500 739 2

Designed and typeset by Guy Croton Publishing Services, West Malling Kent

Printed and bound in India by Parksons Graphics Pvt. Ltd., Mumbai.

CONTENTS

DEDICATION

To Pat Slinn, for a life devoted to BSA and Ducati motorcycles.

Rocket 3 engine in a replica Rob North frame in Parc Fermé at the Manx Grand Prix/ Classic TT.

Detail of an A65-based Norbsa – a Norton Featherbed frame with BSA power.

INTRODUCTION

BSA – or 'The BSA' as those who worked there referred to it – was once the world's most successful motorcycle factory, making more machines than any other in the world by the mid-1950s and employing some 20,000 people. The factory won the 'Queen's Award to Industry' for exports in 1967 and 1968, before collapsing into bankruptcy in 1973. It is an epic rise and fall story, even by the standards of the British motorcycle industry.

My first motorcycle was a BSA, a faded green 249cc C15 registered the day I was born way back in the summer of 1959. My father was convinced we would end our lives together as well, horrified that I'd spent £60 of my own money on a motorcycle with a claimed 70mph performance, rather than step from my Puch M2 moped into the Austin A35 car he'd wanted me to learn to drive in. Of course I was happy to do that when friends with a full car licence needed a lift on a Saturday nights, but I wouldn't pass my car test until three years later, long after I gained a full motorcycle licence and a Suzuki GSX1100. After all, we'd studied George Orwell's *Animal Farm* at school and I was convinced the pigs had got it completely wrong: it was two wheels good, four wheels bad.

But a seventeen-year-old's sympathies tested the C15 to near destruction. All my motorcycle-mad friends had left school at sixteen and fallen into the arms of the Japanese importers and hire purchase. I stayed on for A levels, so had to take what I could on the (very, very) second-hand market. In isolation I loved the C15, but it wouldn't start if it was hot, and the ammeter was lost to a hedgerow as I overtook the school bus one afternoon. And there was no way it could

A warehouse on the far side of the canal, similar to and close to the BSA buildings.

1959 C15 in rather better condition than the author's first motorcycle. ARRIVISTO GREEN

keep up with my friends' oriental quarter-litre lovelies. The C15 went to a pair of lads, who pushed it up and down our street while my younger brothers giggled hysterically. Eventually the lads started it and I had cash in my pocket that would in due course help fund a Honda CB125S.

Then I went on to study business, the course based around the débâcle of a British motorcycle industry run by people who didn't like motorcycles and understood them even less. I became part of a generation that ridiculed their elders' ancient British steeds and embraced everything that BSA's directors didn't think their customers might want: push-button starting, professional dealerships, indicator lights, and the complete reinvention of the wheel at every opportunity.

And yet… as someone who fell in love with Italian motorcycles in general, and Ducatis in particular, I came to re-appreciate the charms of a motorcycle with heritage, and also with that indefinable trait, character. One man single-handedly changed my attitude towards British motorcycles, a man who rose from a plastering apprenticeship to owning a sizeable property empire. John Bloor turned the British motorcycle's last stand at Meriden into a housing estate before plotting Triumph's return. He understood that the revived marque didn't need to be cutting edge but had to be utterly reliable, and have an authenticity that spoke to motorcyclists jaded by Japanese efficacy. His newly commissioned 3-cylinder motor especially was a peach, and the early Speed Triple a star. Bloor even bought himself one of the originals, an X75 Hurricane that was developed by BSA and would have been sold under that banner if history had played out differently.

BSA's first step into life was not a great omen. In June 1861, at a meeting in a Birmingham hotel room, the decision

Pat Slinn on his way to Vienna and an international BSA meeting. Passenger Reg Read used to be an Ariel display rider. COLLECTION OF PAT SLINN

was made to form a public company, The Birmingham Small Arms Company Limited, to manufacture guns. Unfortunately within a few years the market for firearms collapsed, and by 1876 the company faced ruin. It was only a chance encounter with a German immigrant that moved BSA into bicycle production, and ultimately motorcycles. This was initially via building bicycles that could be fitted with imported engines, finally showing an in-house designed and built 498cc side-valve single, listed as the BSA 3.5HP at the 1910 Olympia show. The model sold out for each of the following three years. Within a decade V-twins were added to the range and BSA started to diversify: cars, commercial vehicles, Browning .303s for Spitfires – BSA seemed to rise effortlessly to that number one position.

Pat Slinn with his home-brewed ISDT bike for a *Classic Bike* magazine photoshoot.

Although Honda had overtaken BSA as the world's biggest bike builder as the Swinging Sixties dawned, BSA were far from beaten. Contrary to widespread belief 'The BSA' continued to invest in factories and development, with their finest machines appearing during this period, including the Gold Star and the Rocket III. The latter begat the Hurricane, stolen by Triumph management and today the most valuable of the production BSA/Triumph models.

It was this internal rivalry and associated ill-judged government policy that killed BSA, as it eventually did the rest of the British motorcycle industry. Taxing domestic enterprise at every opportunity while allowing unrestricted imports discouraged investment at home, while it was encouraged in Japan's protected home market. Hubris – a word to be used a lot – meant that neither the British government nor industry saw imports as a threat. Eventually this led to racing victories in the all-important US market being achieved with empty showrooms, bodges to speed up deliveries, and a reputation for disastrous reliability. Panic-stricken directors finally realized they didn't have a grasp of what motorcyclists wanted, and brought in outsiders who knew even less. A glorious slice of British history and industry imploded, leaving the most deserving – the factory workers, suppliers, dealers and motorcyclists – hugely impoverished.

BSA Motorcycles – The Complete Story tells the story of this astounding rise and fall. As well as what became of the factory – it still sits forlorn and unacknowledged at the side of a Birmingham canal –there will be insight from those who worked at the factory, and those who oversaw the Japanese takeover of the industry. The highs – two Maudes Trophies, racing victories, those Queen's awards – will be contrasted with the rapid fall from grace. There will be references to the non-motorcycling production – which included Daimler cars – and a possible future in the ownership of Mahindra, which has hinted at a new range of BSA motorcycles after paying three million pounds for the rights to build them.

In writing this history I owe a very special thanks to three people in particular: world sidecar champion Stan Dibben, who worked at the factory building Gold Stars from 1949 to 1952, and competed and tested for BSA. To Chris Smith, daughter of Jeff, for her insights and introduction to her father; his book, *Jeff Smith: Trials Master, Motocross Maestro* is essential reading. But most of all thanks must go Pat Slinn, a man most famous for his connections to racing Ducatis during the 1970s and 1980s. But Pat started as an apprentice at BSA, and worked in the experimental department as his father had before him. To say he had an insight into the factory is a massive understatement, and without him I could never have written this book.

Gratitude is also due to Gerald Davison, a man who raced a Greeves and then a Honda, before working for Honda, ultimately at director level. Finally a huge thanks to Bonhams for allowing the use of some of the many photographs of motorcycles they have sold.

CHAPTER ONE

BEGINNINGS

There was only one place I could start this story, and try to understand the feelings of those involved in BSA's heyday: Birmingham's Bullring is now a huge temple to those who prefer to worship in a shopping centre, but it was once where Birmingham's motorcyclists congregated. The name comes from the iron hoop to which a bull's nose ring was joined by a length of rope, ready for the auctioneers' gavel. I feel a measure of trepidation when asking about the factory's whereabouts at the Bullring's taxi rank, but needn't have – the driver knows exactly the location of what is left

Armoury Road in 2017.

All roads lead to Birmingham. SIMISI1

of the BSA factory. Almost £10 later I'm standing in front of what was once the biggest motorcycle factory on earth, a surprising stillness around me after the traffic jams of the journey here.

The buildings are still easily recognized, if unloved. One is a car workshop, rammed with discarded bumper panels. At the far end a single-storey building, in red brick like the other original edifices, has bright, polished letters along one side set into blinded windows – BSA: Birmingham Small Arms, advertised as the 'long-established air-rifle manufacturer and retailer, also selling scopes, pellets and silencers'. This is all that's left of a proud history that gave the Armoury Road I'm standing in its name. No blue plaque, no tourist information board, nothing. The canal that runs from the end of the road has recently been refurbished in a multi-million pound investment that failed to find a few pounds to remember what was perhaps Birmingham's finest hour.

Overlooking the canal is another sad and unloved building, gradually decaying, a metaphor for the decline of British industry through the 1960s and 1970s. A sense of entitlement grasped a nation that had been the world leader in innovation, enterprise, and the belief that to be born British was the greatest gift any child could wish for. On the other side of the world the Japanese embraced the post-war possibilities, while Britain – bankrupt and stripped of empire by World War II – was bereft of ambition. Those in the boardroom felt they could return to their unquestioned old world authority, while others, who had seen those men fight, decided it should be the working man who held the levers of power.

'People would come into work with their fishing rods, expecting a walk-out,' remembers Pat Slinn, who, like his father, worked in the experimental department. 'I'd ride my Bantam in round the back to avoid the pickets, but most

These innovative part-reinforced concrete BSA buildings were some of the first of their type in the world. Sadly today they are unloved and used for car repairs.

people just fancied a day off.' Perhaps they should have been more careful of what they wished for. I walk back to the city centre along the beautifully restored – but completely deserted – Grand Union Canal, the smart gravel towpath pleasingly litter free.

Back in the hotel room I email a photo to Chris Smith, daughter of BSA's world champion Jeff. The family lives in Wisconsin close to the great lakes, running *Motorsport Publications* which distributes UK magazines and books to US readers. Chris and Jeff are unequivocal: they never want to see the factory again – it would be just too heart-breaking. I'd met Pat Slinn earlier in the nearby National Motorcycle Museum. After falling silent in the middle of the first hall he stops and raises his hands in the air: 'What happened to it? Where did it all go?' he asks. This is an attempt to find out.

IN THE BEGINNING

Birmingham (originally Bermingehame) means the home of the Beorma, some long-forgotten Anglo-Saxons. By the early twelfth century it had grown into a town, and in 1166, King Henry II gave the Lord of the Manor, Peter De Birmingham, the right to hold a market, which was soon drawing merchants and craftsmen to the area. By the late fourteenth century Birmingham was known for its metalworking, helped by the proximity of iron ore, coal and surrounding streams turning watermills that powered the bellows of the many forges.

In 1570 a writer observed that Birmingham was 'full of inhabitants and echoing with forges', the metalworking industry fast taking over the area. Tudor Birmingham gained a reputation as a place where cutlers made knives, nailers made nails, and blacksmiths worked at their forges. Inevitably this work included making swords and, in turn, an evolution to gunpowder weapons. But each tradesman tended to work alone, and even by the time rifles were being made, there would be specialists for barrels, stocks or even trigger guards. Mass production it was not, and a few men with foresight realized that there needed to be a coming together of like-minded – but variously skilled – smiths.

The Birmingham Small Arms Trade Association gave the city's master gunsmiths a chance to join forces in 1854, with John Dent Goodman elected as chairman the following year. This was a group of men (perhaps as few as fourteen, perhaps as many as twenty-four) intending to supply munitions (particularly handmade muzzle-loading rifles) for the Crimean War.

Presumably the union was successful because, meeting together on the Friday evening of 7 June 1861, the association decided to form a public company, the Birmingham Small Arms Company Limited, in the Gun Quarter of England's second city, with Goodman remaining chairman. The War Office promised the BSA gunsmiths free access to technical drawings and to the War Office's Board of Ordnance's Royal Small Arms factory at Enfield – as in Royal Enfield. New machinery developed in the United States (US) had been installed at Enfield, and greatly increased output without needing more skilled craftsmen.

The great and the good of Birmingham viewed the expansion of Enfield with suspicion, knowing that the dedicated factory's proximity to London and its long history of producing firearms gave it an advantage over the loose-knit gunsmiths of Birmingham. Throughout the evolution of the British rifle the name 'Enfield' is prevalent, meaning the Royal Small Arms Factory in the town – now suburb – of Enfield – hence its eventual renaming as 'Royal Enfield'. This factory, north of London, was where the British government had produced muskets since 1804.

The first British repeating rifle was developed in 1879, and adopted as the Magazine Rifle Mark I in 1888, commonly referred to as the Lee-Metford. 'Lee' was James Paris Lee,

Birmingham's canals are used for leisure today, but were essential to the city's prosperity. WONJONG OH

Lee-Metford Mk II .303. ARMÉMUSEUM / SWEDISH ARMY MUSEUM

a Scottish-born Canadian-American inventor who designed an easy-to-operate turn bolt and magazine to work with it. 'Metford' was William Ellis Metford, an Englishman instrumental in perfecting the smaller .303 calibre – the calibre of the Spitfire's Brownings. These developments led to the Lee-Enfield repeating rifle, which served as the British Empire and Commonwealth's main firearm during the first half of the twentieth century. It was also the British Army's standard rifle from its adoption in 1895 until 1957, so if Birmingham couldn't persuade the government to allow them to be part of the project, its firearms industry was doomed.

The BSA's stated purpose on establishment in 1861 was to make guns by machinery and, although no mention is made of it, the only significant conflict by this time was the American Civil War, the Crimean War having ended in 1856. This would prove the fallibility of building a city's future around weaponry: there are times in history when wars are thankfully rare, and they are often unpredictable. BSA, like Royal Enfield, would have to find an alternative revenue stream, and they would both fall upon the same idea: the motorcycle.

BSA settled on a 25-acre (10-hectare) site at Small Heath on the condition that the Great Western Railway would build a station nearby. By 1863 the factory was complete, standing alone in open countryside, a square, red-brick fortress with towers at each corner, apparently mainly employing women, judging by photographs of the era. It was set south of the Coventry road and what is now the A45, to the south-west of the city centre and squeezed between the new Small Heath train station and one of the final sections of the Grand Union Canal, which absorbed the older Warwick and Birmingham Junction Canal. This ensured swift loading and excellent links to Manchester and London, as well as to the ports of Liverpool and Bristol.

When you visit Birmingham it's never long before a proud local will tell you that 'Birmingham has more miles of canal than Venice'. Is this true? The exact numbers depend on where you draw the city boundaries, but the system adds up to around 100 miles (160km) of canals. It was certainly one of the most intricate canal networks in the world, the life-blood of Victorian Birmingham and the Black Country. At their height, the canals were so busy that gas lighting was installed beside the locks to permit round-the-clock operation. Boats were built without cabins for maximum carrying capacity, and a near-tidal effect arose from swarms of narrowboats converging on the Black Country collieries at the same time each day.

In 1866 BSA acquired a munitions factory in Adderley Park, about two miles (3km) north of the Small Heath site and again between a train station and a waterway, this time the Birmingham and Warwick Junction Canal, which connected to the Warwick and Birmingham Junction Canal. This allowed BSA to fulfil a government order to upgrade 100,000 muzzle-loading Enfield rifles. In 1873 the Adderley Park Rolling Mills became home to the Birmingham Small Arms and Metal Company, to fulfil an order from the Prussian army. Following the government's switch to the Martini-Henry rifle in 1871, BSA followed suit, producing these from 1874.

Unfortunately the demand for firearms collapsed as peace became established around the world, leaving the founding fathers of BSA's business plan in tatters. By 1876 they faced ruin, and on 19 August 1878, the factory closed and remained shut for a year until a small order for guns encouraged the managers to reopen. They also sought diversification, realizing that being entirely reliant on one product – firearms – was foolhardy. This attitude of seeking out new products and markets would come to define BSA, ironically until a focus on two very particular motorcycles precipitated its demise.

THE FIRST TWO-WHEELED BSAS

Happily, in 1880 a slightly odd visitor came to the factory, one Edward Carl Fredrich Otto, who had built a novel type of bicycle with a large wheel on each side of the rider, rather than in front of and behind the saddle. He had been introduced by Messrs Smith and Lamb of Ipswich, with a request to manufacture his Otto Patent Safety Dicycle (rather than bicycle). BSA's directors allowed Otto to demonstrate the 'dicycle' by lifting it on to the boardroom table and riding back and forth, while he explained how to balance the machine and the oddball steering. He completed his party piece by riding down the staircase and into the street.

It was a historic moment, and the directors were convinced that the future of BSA lay with the production of road transport. They agreed to manufacture the Otto dicycle, and on 2 July 1880, a contract was agreed for BSA to build 210 at £8 15s each, less tyres, the first being delivered on 20 September. Despite this first contract resulting in a loss, a second contract was agreed to supply 200 Ottos at £13 each, with tyres. In all, a total of 953 machines were built and sold by the Otto Bicycle Company of 118 Newgate Street, London, at £21 apiece.

So having diversified into bicycle building, BSA introduced its own design the following year before adding tricycles to the range. These were branded with badges carrying the three crossed guns, which, although it had been used within BSA for some time, only became officially registered in

Advertisement for the Otto Dicycle.

Unknown sampler of an Otto Dicycle circa 1882.

1881. This 'piled rifle' trademark was to become a familiar sight throughout the world, an instant explanation of a huge motorcycle factory's origin.

In August 1885 – the year Bianchi was founded, still famous for its bicycles – BSA was awarded a bronze medal for their safety bicycle at the International Inventions Exhibition, and BSA's production of so-called safety (that is, easy to stay aboard compared to the Penny Farthing) bicycles, and tricycles, steadily increased. But in 1887, the government – more specifically the British Empire's – demand for rifles and ammunition was such that the company abandoned bicycle and tricycle manufacture. The people at the top of BSA were gunsmiths and, to free factory floor space to build more Lee-Metford rifles, between 1888 and 1893 BSA returned to its roots, turning production over entirely to the magazine rifle. But within five years, the market for armaments collapsed once again and a return to bicycles was contemplated.

Bicycle sales had skyrocketed while BSA had been away, thanks to the invention in 1887 of the pneumatic tyre. John Dunlop was a Scottish vet working with his brother James in Downpatrick, south of Belfast, who first made pneumatic tyres for his child's tricycle before developing them for bicycle racing. He sold his rights for a modest sum, unaware how pivotal his invention would be, his only reward being a sort of immortality as his name remained when the Dunlop Rubber Company was established in Birmingham in 1901.

BACK TO BICYCLES

By a stroke of good fortune a Mr George – apparently known as Billy – Illston called at the BSA factory to see his friend Mr Clements about a billiards match, and noticed that some of the shell-making plant was idle. He urged his friend, and anyone else at BSA who would listen to him, to use the redundant machinery to make bicycle parts. In return he would become the company's first commercial traveller, living solely on the commission he earned. So early in 1893, BSA started to make bicycle hubs, examples of which were exhibited at the Crystal Palace Show later in the year.

By November 1893 Illston was working full time for BSA, selling hubs and other components across the country. The trade price of hubs was 15s (shillings) (75p) per pair in dozen lots; Brown Brothers of London contracted for 2,000 pairs. Success came quickly. People used to the precision of gun making did not relax their standards when they turned to other work, and the BSA hubs were soon joined by bottom brackets, chain wheels and other parts, which were soon acknowledged as the finest available. It was these components that built BSA's early reputation for quality.

As the cycling boom continued, more buildings sprouted up at the Small Heath site, soon doubling the factory's floor space. In the first decade of the twentieth century the expansion continued, BSA now very much a bicycle maker in the public's imagination.

Then in 1902, Triumph launched their first motorcycle, expanding rapidly from bicycle production with funding from Dunlop tyres. The vehicle was an immediate hit, powered by a single-cylinder four-stroke Belgian Minerva engine with automatic inlet valve and battery/coil ignition, clipped to the downtube of a Triumph bicycle frame.

Minerva had started out manufacturing bicycles in 1897, before expanding into light cars and motorized bicycles in 1900. It might be hard to believe now, but Belgium was at the forefront of the internal combustion engine's development, its head start destroyed by World War I. The company took its name from the Roman goddess of wisdom and strategy, and as the sponsor of arts and – most importantly – trade. They produced lightweight clip-on engines that were mounted below the bicycle front down tube, specifically for Minerva bicycles, but also available in kit form suitable for almost any bicycle. The engine drove a belt that turned a large gear wheel attached to the side of the rear wheel opposite to the chain. In 1901 the kit engine was a 211cc unit allowing comfortable cruising at around 20mph (30km/h), and half as much again on full throttle.

In these pioneering days the horsepower rating was not as universal as it is today, where the quoted brake horsepower (bhp) is a measure of an engine's ability to turn a brake of some sort. While this empirical measurement was available to engineers from the birth of the internal combustion engine, British tax authorities at least insisted on a theoretical calculation based upon the engine's specification, determined by the RAC in the UK. This equated one horsepower equal to 2sq in (12.9sq cm) of piston area, and came to be known as the Treasury Rating. Perhaps even more oddly, manufacturers would list models by this rating rather than give them a name: it was the 1930s before this really changed, and even the fabulous Coventry Eagle Flying Eight was thus named after its RAC 8 HP rating, despite producing around 30bhp.

Thus while Minerva claimed 1.5bhp at 1,500rpm, the motor was rated at 2.25HP in the UK. These kits to turn

1904 Minerva-powered BSA in the National Motorcycle Museum.

bicycles into powered two-wheelers were exported as far as Australia. Minerva struggled to build on their early success, hampered – hammered even – by two world wars and the Depression, but were still making Land Rovers under licence for the Belgium army as late as 1956.

Triumph sold 500 of their Minerva-powered motorcycles in 1903, and started prototyping with British JAP (John Alfred Prestwich) motors for an expanded range. The same year BSA experimented with a motorcycle with a BSA pattern frame fitted with a Minerva 233cc engine, similar to the contemporary Triumph's. Yet, initially at least, BSA seemed happy to supply frames and rolling chassis for others to bolt Minerva engines on to. Instead, BSA set about designing and developing their own motor in house, a long gestation period indicative of how they wanted to be certain it would be reliable, economical and fast enough to become the market leader.

In 1906 BSA took over the former National Arms and Ammunition Company's (aka the Royal Small Arms) factory in Sparkbrook, and a year later the Eadie Manufacturing Company in Redditch, makers of cycle parts almost as famous as BSA's. This would prove to be a BSA trait – buying up the local competition. In 1910 BSA acquired the Daimler Motor Company just as they were about to enter the motorcycle business.

BSA CARS BEAT MOTORCYCLES INTO PRODUCTION

Dudley Docker – father of the later (in)famous Sir Bernard – joined BSA's board in 1906 and was appointed deputy chairman in 1909. He had made a spectacular financial success of a merger of five large rolling-stock companies in 1902, and so became the leader of the period's merger movement. Believing he could buy in the missing management skills lacking within BSA, he started merger talks with Daimler in Coventry. Daimler, alongside Rover, was then the biggest British car builder, and immensely profitable. The attraction for Daimler shareholders in joining forces with BSA was its apparent stability. So in 1910, BSA purchased Daimler with BSA shares – but Docker, who brokered the deal, either ignored or failed to predict the outcome of the pairing.

Nothing was seemingly done to make the factories work together, the two remaining separate and almost wilfully uncooperative: hints of what was to come when BSA absorbed Triumph. Docker officially 'retired' as a BSA director in 1912 following a 1909 report on the merger by BSA's investigation committee, although he was allowed to install Lincoln Chandler as his replacement. In 1913 Daimler

Torpedo-bodied 3309cc Daimler, first registered in December 1913. CHARLES 01

employed 5,000 workers to manufacture just 1,000 vehicles, an indication that things were not well. And BSA continued to produce cars of their own, some using Daimler engines.

From 1907 to 1914 BSA built a range of six cars in various forms, but all with steel bodies and rear-wheel drive, powered by 4-cylinder engines ranging from 2596cc to 5401cc. Production started in 1907 with the 18/23HP, joined by the range-topping 25/33HP between 1908 and 1911. The larger models were based on the 1907 Peking-Paris Itala, the car that had won the race of the same name. It was an astounding and rightly celebrated race, starting at the French embassy in Peking on 10 June 1907, with winner Prince Scipione Borghese's Itala arriving in Paris on 10 August.

In 1910 BSA's range gained the 15/20HP and 20/25HP cars – really just re-badged Daimlers – and in 1912 all car production was transferred to Daimler's Coventry home, the range reduced to a single model, the 13.9HP with a 4-cylinder 2015cc motor, also briefly sold by Siddeley-Deasy with a different radiator cover as the Stoneleigh. The bodies built at Sparkbrook were among the first to be all metal, while BSA/Daimler also supplied engines, gearboxes and rear axles for other Siddeley-Deasy cars. In 1914 war stopped car production, although BSA would return to four- (and three-) wheelers in 1921.

THE FIRST BSA MOTORCYCLE

Meanwhile Triumph, a few miles down the road and close to BSA's car factory at Coventry, had proved the value of motorcycle manufacture. They had moved swiftly to develop the idea of a bicycle frame with a Minerva engine, and were soon building 1,000 motorcycles a year in a new, purpose-built factory. By 1905 there were 21,121 motorcycles registered in the UK, and in 1908 Triumph launched their first motorcycle designed and built completely in house. Its 300cc motor was rated at 3HP and offered a 45mph (72km/h) top speed, three times what a horse and carriage could manage. By 1910 Triumph were building 3,000 motorcycles a year, and the company's founder, Siegfried Bettmann, had become

Older restoration of a 1913 model, very similar to the original 1910 BSA 3.5HP. YESTERDAYS ANTIQUE MOTORCYCLES

The original BSA 3.5HP TT (Tourist Trophy) model of 1910–1913 in period.

BSA 3.5HP

Year: 1911
Displacement: 499cc
Bore/stroke: 85 x 88mm
Engine type: Four-stroke side valve
Cylinders: 1
Weight: 91kg (201lb)
Top speed: 45mph (72km/h)

Birmingham's mayor and a British citizen. However, his German heritage loomed large and he felt compelled to stand down once war seemed inevitable.

And so finally in 1910, BSA entered the lucrative and prestigious motorcycle market with a single model that would remain a standard for many years to come, reflecting the quality of materials and design. This first model had a vertical single-cylinder 3.5HP engine, with a chain-driven magneto, sprung forks and the excellent finish associated with BSA's bicycles. Within six months from launch, BSA's new motorcycle was selling well, the machines easily distinguishable from rival marques with their yellow and green-painted tanks. A rear-hub, two-speed gearbox was soon added.

First shown at the 1910 Olympia Show, London, for the 1911 season, the entire production run sold out in 1911, 1912 and 1913. Initially priced at £50, it was also available with a 'free' engine, referring to the double cone clutch in the rear hub at £56 10s (£56 50p). To put these prices in perspective, in 1910 average annual earnings were around £70 for men and £30 for women working a fifty-five-hour week.

In 1913 Kenneth Holden, BSA's chief test rider, won the company's first race on what was claimed to be a standard production 3.5HP model at Brooklands, averaging 60.75mph (97.77km/h). The following year, six of eight BSA entrants finished the Senior TT races. The 1914 meeting was the first to make crash helmets compulsory, and was also the first to start at the top of Bray Hill, close to the current starting point on Glencrutchery Road. BSA's best result was a twelfth place for one D. Young in a race dominated by Cyril Pullin's Rudge.

For 1915 BSA offered a choice between the original 499cc 85 x 88mm 3.5HP model and the long-stroke 556cc 85 x

From the final year of the original Model K run in 1916. BENJAMIN HEALLEY/ MUSEUMVICTORIA

The Model K still looks remarkably similar to BSA's first 3.5HP model, proof that the design was pretty much right first time. RODNEY START/MUSEUMSVICTORIA

98mm 4.25HP Model H. This latter was advertised as being especially suitable for sidecar work, now available directly from BSA for the first time. The Model H also had the three-speed BSA gearbox with foot-controlled clutch that was introduced in 1914, and a twin-barrel BSA carburettor. Both models could be had in a chain-cum-belt version or in all chain drive with encased chains, which made the machine £3 5s (£3 25p) more expensive.

The 1913 3.5HP models A, B, C, D and E were all now also available in France, along with three versions of BSA's Duco sidecars. For 1915 the 556cc 4.25HP model could be had with a three-speed gearbox and, although this Model K production ceased in 1916, it resumed after the war and continued into the 1920s. Development continued with other models joining the range, including the three-speed chain-cum-belt model 'K' and the all-chain model 'H', as well as several well designed sidecars. Until well into the 1930s, various versions of this model were added, adapted or, inevitably, discontinued.

BSA dropped civilian motorcycle manufacture during World War I, focusing on their traditional manufacture of guns. 1914 would have been a frenetic year at BSA even without the war. The bicycles and motorcycles were popular, with worldwide demand expected to exceed the previous year. The first prototype car had been produced in 1907, on sale the following year, marketed under the BSA Cycles banner. The company sold 150 in 1909, but it is clear that the new diversification was considered unsuccessful, as an investigation committee reporting to the main board listed many failures of management and poorly organized production of the cars. This led to the successful bid for the Daimler car factory, although the two marques remained separate.

However, the arms department remained flat out fulfilling government orders, one of the most important being for the US-designed Lewis machine gun, for which the company held sole European manufacturing rights. Unsurprisingly this demand continued throughout World War I.

1922 BSA 556cc Model H. BONHAMS

The average BSA production for the years prior to the war had been some 135 weapons each week. By the peak of the war 10,000 rifles were leaving Armoury Road every week, including, by the end of the first industrial-scale war in history, 145,000 Lewis machine guns. This massive increase in production called for factory extensions, with three new four-storey blocks rising at the end of Armoury Road. In 1915 work commenced on a four-storey 'New' building for Lewis gun manufacture, expanding BSA's portfolio to five factories. Anyone walking the full length of each of the 60ft (18m) wide workshops would cover a total of two miles (3.2km).

Other equipment produced for the military included motorcycles, the first folding bicycles, machine tools, aircraft components, gun locks, shells and fuses. Daimler supplied most of the cars, ambulances and commercial vehicles to the military, including the engine and transmission of the world's first tank. At the peak of the war the factories owned by the BSA group were employing nearly 20,000 people, compared with the pre-war total of 6,500.

After the Armistice it was decided to put the company's three main activities under separate management, and so three new subsidiaries were formed. BSA Cycles handled bicycle and motorcycle production at Small Heath and Redditch; BSA Guns continued small arms work at Small Heath; and BSA Tools worked in the Sparkbrook factory at the business of small tools, jigs and special-purpose machines. Daimler remained a separate entity, albeit under BSA's ownership and answerable to BSA's main board.

Before World War I, Britain had been the world's economic superpower. With rapid growth and a vast empire, the country benefitted from significant wealth and resources, but still wasn't ready for the economic impact of the biggest conflict in history. When the war erupted in the

BSA-built Lewis MKI light machine gun, circa 1914. P1914 Pattern, .303in calibre, gas-operated. COLLECTION OF AUCKLAND MUSEUM TAMAKI PAENGA HIRA, W1492

summer of 1914, Britain faced market panic and an unprecedented financial crisis. Not only did the government need to reassure the markets, it had to prepare itself for the almost unimaginable economic demands of war on an industrial scale, a scale never seen before in terms of either monetary or human cost.

The government turned to direct taxes – on property and income – on a far greater scale than ever before. In 1913 income tax was only paid by 2 per cent of the population, but during the war another 2.4 million people became liable, so that by 1918, four times as many people were paying income tax as before the war. How this money was spent – or used to repay loans – was therefore now decided by government rather than the people who earned it.

There was also massive borrowing from the public through the war bonds scheme, only repaid in 2014 when historically low interest rates meant the fixed 3.5 per cent paid on war bonds finally looked high: the same rate had been paid through the 1970s and early eighties, when inflation ran at over 20 per cent. The government had also cut itself free from the Gold Standard with the Currency and Bank Notes Act of 1914, which enabled the Bank of England to increase the amount of money available simply by printing it, even though this risked inflation and so rising prices.

So although Britain was ultimately victorious, the effects of war would be felt for many years. Foreign trade, a key part of the British economy, had been badly damaged, with countries cut off from the supply of British goods. This allowed countries not affected by the war to build up their own industries and so they were no longer reliant on Britain, instead directly competing with her. So by 1920 Britain was experiencing the deepest recession in her history. The public were hit by higher taxes, the effective confiscation of savings when war bonds weren't repaid, rising prices, and the loss of jobs and earnings with the collapse of exports. It was into this world that BSA, like many others, had to sell their products.

CHAPTER TWO

TROPHY CHASING – AND A THING FOR CARS

The post-war BSA group might have seemed a strong, well balanced business with a wide range of products, but the high hopes for 1919 were soon dashed. Two years later, half of the group's labour force had gone, although there were bright spots in the economic doom and gloom. BSA's motorcycle range was proving so popular that the advertising slogan 'One in four is a BSA' was adopted, with BSA building more motorcycles than the rest of British industry put together. These were all based on the original 1910 3.5HP 499cc single until the arrival of BSA's first V-twin in 1919 (for the 1920 season), sold as a motorcycle with reasonable, rather than exceptional, performance.

In the months leading up to World War I, BSA had been working on a V-twin project, suspended when the conflict began. However, its post-war revival gave BSA a product for the return of veterans who had enjoyed their first experience of the motorcycle, albeit under the shadow of war. Initially listed as the Model A V-twin, it was renamed simply Model E from 1921; most were supplied with a BSA sidecar. This was the first of a line of BSAs with a 771cc engine rated officially at 6 or 7HP, featuring BSA's own three-speed gearbox and an aluminium alloy chain case. The front and rear wheels were the same size and interchangeable so that a spare could usefully be carried on the sidecar. Despite chain drive, the wheels appeared to have dummy belt rims, which were actually for the brake friction levers.

The 50-degree angle of the V layout was a compromise, giving adequate space between the cylinders for cooling, but

BSA's first V-twin – the 770cc (6/7 HP) Model E appeared late in 1919. This one was first registered on 28 January 1921. BONHAMS

Australia's MuseumVictoria has some wonderful archive images, sadly with little known beyond the print. This is from circa 1925. MUSEUMVICTORIA

Another from the MuseumVictoria, with a BSA apparently offering a fine family day out. MUSEUMVICTORIA

allowing a shorter wheelbase than the perfect balance of a 90-degree layout. The emphasis was on torque for sidecar work and reliability, together with ease of maintenance. The machine was a success, and its descendants continued in production until the outbreak of World War II. The Light 6 [HP], introduced in 1923, was a budget version of the Model E, with various components lightened or removed in order to reduce production costs. However, the lower weight made it popular as a solo machine, and it outlived its heavier brother – now listed as the Deluxe – by two years. BSA stressed the reliability of their machines, the availability of spares and dealer support, aiming to appeal to as many riders as possible rather than just the wealthy enthusiast to whom others – notably Brough Superior – were selling. Nonetheless, to the vast majority of British citizens the BSA still looked to be a lot of money.

The BSA Model E side valve V-twins architecture involved a bore and stoke of 76 x 85mm to give 771cc, using mechanical pump lubrication with an emergency hand plunger. The modest 6/7HP produced by the engine was able to provide a top speed of 55–60mph (89–97km/h). Despite being an extravagance, there was an increased demand for transport after the end of the war and the Model E became popular, especially when matched to BSA's matching green and cream-painted sidecar. Retail price was £130 – a lot of money when £4 a week was a decent wage, but a comparative bargain when the basic Austin Twenty car cost £595.

Designed for easy servicing, the valves as well as the wheels were interchangeable, and had quickly adjustable tappets. Other features included an Amac carburettor, chain drive, choice of magneto or magdyno, seven plate clutch, and a kick starter driving through the gearbox.

The Model E would prove the forerunner of a long line of rugged and dependable sidecar tugs. A larger, 80 × 99mm 985cc 8HP version made its debut as the Model F in 1922, and would continue in production as the Model G, regularly revised and updated, until 1940. In the days when cars were almost unspeakably expensive, family motoring did not get better than this: a powerful V-twin with a rugged three-speed gearbox carried in a well-built heavyweight frame and hauling a substantial sidecar complete with luggage compartment and full weather protection.

Between 1920 and 1925 BSA produced 100 small three-wheeled taxi cabs using the Model E 771cc motor, and a 1919 BSA Model E complete with matching sidecar featured in a car chase in the 1965 movie *Those Magnificent Men in Their Flying Machines*, driven by lead actor Stuart Whitman playing American cowboy Orvil Newton.

ABOVE: **This V-twin was one of nineteen motorcycle taxis plying their trade in Birmingham, whose Hackney Carriage Authority was one of the few that allowed sidecars to be used in this way.** BONHAMS

The County Cycle and Motor Co. of Broad Street, Birmingham, sold these outfits with the Mead and Deakin 'Canoelet' sidecar for £252 14s 8d. The meter drive was listed as an extra, while the meter itself could be hired for £8 per annum. BONHAMS

THE MODEL E

Year: 1921
Displacement: 771cc
Bore/stroke: 76 x 85mm
Engine type: Four-stroke side-valve
Cylinders: 2
Weight: 191kg (421lb)
Top speed: 55–60mph (89–97km/h)

But the V-twin was never going to be a big seller at over £100 new, even when it grew to almost a full litre in capacity, largely to make it even more suitable for chair work. This larger 986cc version made its debut as the Model F in 1922, and would continue in production as the Model G until 1940. Even so, the changes made to the big V-twin during the 1930s were few compared with those made to BSA's singles: but then, they served a much broader customer base.

THE COST OF RIDING

The main costs associated with owning a motorcycle was very much down to the purchase price and fuel economy. The Finance Act 1920 added a 'Duty on licences for mechanically propelled vehicles', which was to be hypothecated – that is, the revenue would be exclusively dedicated to a particular expenditure, namely the newly established Road Fund. Excise duties specifically for mechanically propelled vehicles were first imposed in 1921, along with the requirement to display a vehicle licence (tax disc). Third party insurance wouldn't become compulsory until introduced with the Road Traffic Act 1930, and compulsory testing was not introduced until 1936: even then, passing the driving test allowed the licence holder to drive most things, even if he (and it usually was a 'he') had simply been observed riding a motorcycle around a city square. And learners on a so-called provisional (but easily renewed) licence wouldn't be limited to 250cc until 1961. Until then the only reason to own a small-capacity motorcycle was purchase price, perhaps combined with a need for good fuel economy. A low horsepower rating also helped keep taxes low.

BSA's response was the 349cc 2.75HP 1923 Model L, one of the final flat-tank models. It was available with either a side- or overhead-valve motor, virtually half the V-twin but with a notably longer stroke at 72 x 85.5mm. The overhead-valve version was the company's first such model, but it otherwise shared all of its running gear with its side-valve stablemate, including a three-speed, hand-change, constant-mesh gearbox, an Amac carburettor and chain final drive. Front and rear brakes were friction pads rubbing on dummy rims built into the wheel spokes. Although lubrication was achieved with a mechanical oil pump, the rider could adjust the oil flow depending upon the engine's demands with a tank-mounted adjuster that included a sight glass.

Excise duties for 'mechanically propelled vehicles' were first imposed in 1921, along with the requirement to display a vehicle licence (tax disc). This early example is on a BSA 250 'Round Tank'. BONHAMS

A 1924 BSA Model L 350 stands in the shadow of an Avro Lancaster with Browning machine guns in the turrets, most likely also made by BSA. J. BELL

The side-valve Model L was immediately successful. According to *Pitman's Book of The BSA*: 'To the sporting solo rider who asks for a "go anywhere" mount, its records in the Scottish Six Day Trial and the International trials in Sweden in 1923 stand as recommendation.' When new in the UK, a side-valve Model L cost £47 10s, which was still a lot of money.

THE ROUND TANK – A 250 FOR ALL

So, reflecting the dreadful economic circumstances of the 1920s, mass-production methods were introduced at BSA motorcycles for the first time in 1924 with the introduction of the sturdy little 249cc 'Round Tank' B25 model: this sold at just £37 15s, at a time when a buying a new bicycle would rarely give change from £10. Not surprisingly the quarter-litre BSA was an immediate hit, and used by just about every tradesman who required cheap transport. Popular with learners – the fact that the gearbox had only two speeds and that both brakes operated on the rear wheel were attributes guaranteed to comfort novices – the reliable 250 side-valve provided many with their first motorcycle.

Advanced features, for a lightweight, included primary and final chain drive, and pumped lubrication, although the

THE ROUND TANK MODEL B25

Year: 1924
Displacement: 249cc
Bore/stroke: 63 x 80mm
Engine type: Four-stroke side-valve
Cylinders: 1
Weight: 77kg (177lb)
Top speed: 45mph (72km/h)

A 1924 BSA 'Round Tank', the reason for the name obvious in comparison to earlier 'flat tanks', a label that was only used retrospectively. BONHAMS

Close-up of the Round Tank. The valves' chamber and spark plug can be seen to be on the far side of the cylinder, hence this is called a side-valve motor. BONHAMS

traditional sight feed and auxiliary hand pump remained. A three-speed version – identifiable by its black tank – was added for 1926, and then the following year a wedge-shaped tank replaced the 'round' original. Options included acetylene lighting, EIC magneto, AMAC carburettor and a bulb horn.

Shortly after its launch, four of these BSA 250s made motorcycling history by successfully climbing Snowdon. This was a common motoring publicity stunt back in motoring's early history, if understandably illegal now. BSA were consolidating their position as the default choice amongst motorcycle buyers, reaping rewards for setting their sails against the storm of the post-war economic collapse. When a booming motorcycle market finally returned, BSA were able to dominate in a way that no other British factory could claim to have done. Their lightweight 250cc single was very much a new venture for BSA, entering what was known to be a difficult market because, historically, the public had been treated to many poorly designed and under-engineered bargain buckets from other makers. BSA realized that while a 250 had to be cheap, it also had to trustworthy. This was a market sector where buyers needed reliable transport, despite not having much to spend.

As a result the smallest BSA to date was utterly conventional, with a side-valve four-stroke engine in place of the often unreliable and problematic two-stroke. The Round

A 1927 BSA Model B Deluxe. CRAIG HOWELL

Tank was strong enough to take all (most?) an uncaring rider might throw at it, and it was cheap, despite belt-and-braces lubrication, with oil in the front section of the cylindrical combined oil and fuel tank that gave the model its nickname. The mudguards must have been some of the widest ever fitted to a motorcycle, capable of protecting the rider in the foulest conditions, in fact so wide that the front forks actually passed through them. Primary and final drive was chain, with the gearbox operated by a long hand lever.

With such a concern for practicality it might seem odd that the BSA factory didn't offer a front brake, but these often troubled new riders, worried that they might lock the front wheel and crash. BSA's design team also felt that, with such a modest top speed, a back brake should be perfectly adequate. But BSA's new lightweight coincided with a new legal requirement that all vehicles should be fitted with two independent means of stopping, so there was also a friction block operated by a handlebar lever that pressed on the dummy belt rim on the rear wheel.

The resulting bike was pleasant enough – utility transport that continued to build on BSA's reputation for quality and reliability. The Mount Snowdon publicity stunt, in May 1924, to climb the Welsh mountain in just over half an hour, was conducted alongside the railway track that ran to the top. The feat helped the Round Tank sell in large numbers – some 35,000 – and contributed to its being adopted by the Post Office for telegram delivery. This remained a familiar role for BSA lightweights for many years, right up to the era of the BSA Bantam and the twilight years of the company.

HUMILIATION AT THE TT LEADS TO MAUDES TROPHY AMBITIONS

BSA were to embrace proof of endurance and the capabilities of their production models, rather than pursue the 'win on Sunday, sell on Monday' approach of almost all other manufacturers. The race most manufacturers dreamed of winning was the Isle of Man TT, especially the Senior. BSA was no different, until a disastrous attempt to dominate the event in 1921. While most riders and manufacturers believed that racing – and ideally winning – was essential to the development of motorcycles, BSA became the 'exception that proves the rule': they would instead focus on off-road competition and endurance awards such as the Maudes Trophy, following that humiliating TT.

BSA had secured a works entry for the 1921 Senior TT, building fourteen works 500cc bikes and engaging six suitably fêted riders. After much testing at Brooklands the bikes were shipped to the island in BSA's trademark green and cream livery. But the Brooklands tests, extensive as they were, had not replicated the unique conditions of a 226-mile (364km) TT, and the BSAs did not handle well on the demanding Manx roads, with one rider, Gus Kuhn, sidelined by injuries during practice. Not one of the machines starting the race even made the half-way mark, with problems such as valve failures and melted pistons ending BSA's Isle of Man ambitions. The incident shook BSA, which would have nothing more to do with road racing – and the Isle of Man in particular – for many years. Even as late as the mid-1950s, the BSA board were extremely wary of racing on tarmac.

So the 250 Round Tank's 1924 Snowdon exploit became a template for BSA's attempts to impress potential buyers. It was eclipsed two years later, with BSA's first Maudes Trophy win. This Auto Cycle Union-administered prize, one of the toughest tests of a motorcycle, required a manufacturer to use randomly chosen parts from an assembly line to build a production bike. After a brief inspection, the machines were ridden across Europe, taking part in competitions, tests and time trails, and ridden back to the factory. There were failures galore.

The Maudes Trophy is a silver cup donated in 1923 by George Pettyt, owner of Maudes Motor Mart, based in Great Portland Street, London, to promote impartially judged endurance tests for production motorcycles to prove exceptional reliability. His intention was for an annual award, although over the years the award has proved to be infrequent, the ACU insisting that it was only conferred for outstanding achievements: BSA's first was with a 1926 demonstration of sixty climbs of Bwlcb-Y-Groes. There would be two more years in which BSA would again be awarded the trophy, in 1938 and 1952.

The next feat of endurance that BSA pursued in the search for publicity and sales was when John Castley and Bertram Cathrick embarked on a world tour aboard BSA V-twins. Two 986cc Colonial Model Gs equipped with sidecars set out in August 1926 on a tour through twenty-four countries, completing the tour successfully in March 1928 having covered 25,000 miles (40,225km) including sailings. They crossed the Andes, completing 20,000 land miles (32,000km) on their eighteen-month marathon. More achievements were chalked up in the Thirties, when the reli-

Ready to tour the world: a 986cc 1932 BSA Model G32-14. BONHAMS

A proud owner gets ready to run their Sloper on the Classic TT /Manx Grand Prix parade lap of the Isle of Man.

able new 'Slopers' gave way to the sporting Blue Stars and Empire Stars, which made their mark in trials and clubman events.

In 1925 BSA Motorcycles became a separate, private company, but the march to world domination by the main board continued. In 1926 BSA joined up with Standard Telephones and Cables – formerly Western-Electric – to develop 'broadcast receiving apparatus': the resulting BSA Radio Ltd was based at Small Heath.

In the early 1920s BSA had co-opted engineer and designer Harold Briggs from Daimler, who was responsible for the first overhead-valve BSA, the L28, which was added to the range in 1924. The 72mm x 85.5mm 348cc single-cylinder engine was a spin-off from the Hotchkiss 90-degree V-twin: this was a French marque that had hurriedly relocated to Coventry as World War I approached. From his time at Daimler, Briggs was familiar with the design, which would also be used to power the BSA Light 10 car, when BSA returned to that market in 1921.

Briggs' new single-cylinder engine had fully enclosed valve gear with automatic lubrication, something taken for granted now, but pioneer riders expected to operate hand pumps to feed oil to their engines. These total loss systems lubricated the engine first and the road and rider second, with many fitted with sight feeds to allow a rider to be certain the engine was getting its oil. Briggs' L28 not only retained sight feeds, but also included a hand pump for 'emergencies' such as particularly steep hills. The maximum power output from the engine in sports trim using the optional high-compression piston was reportedly now 13bhp, giving it a top speed of 60mph (97km/h). Note that the nominal power for tax purposes was still just 3.5HP. If the claimed brake horsepower figure is correct, it certainly shows just how quickly the 'tax' calculation was overtaken by advances in engineering, given that BSA's original 3.5HP could manage just 45mph (72km/h).

Briggs continued to design a range of new sporting machines for BSA, including their popular Model S, a 493cc overhead-valve Sloper launched in 1927 for the 1928 season. Some have written that the 'S' designation stood for Sloper, but the model name had been used previously on vertical singles, and the 556cc Deluxe version was listed as the Model H. Inclining the cylinder some 30 degrees forwards brought a number of benefits: the exhaust valve, often the most fragile component in an engine, was better

BSA Sloper 500 with Barbara Davies and Billy Gall aboard, c. 1938 in Blackall, Queensland. STATE LIBRARY OF QUEENSLAND

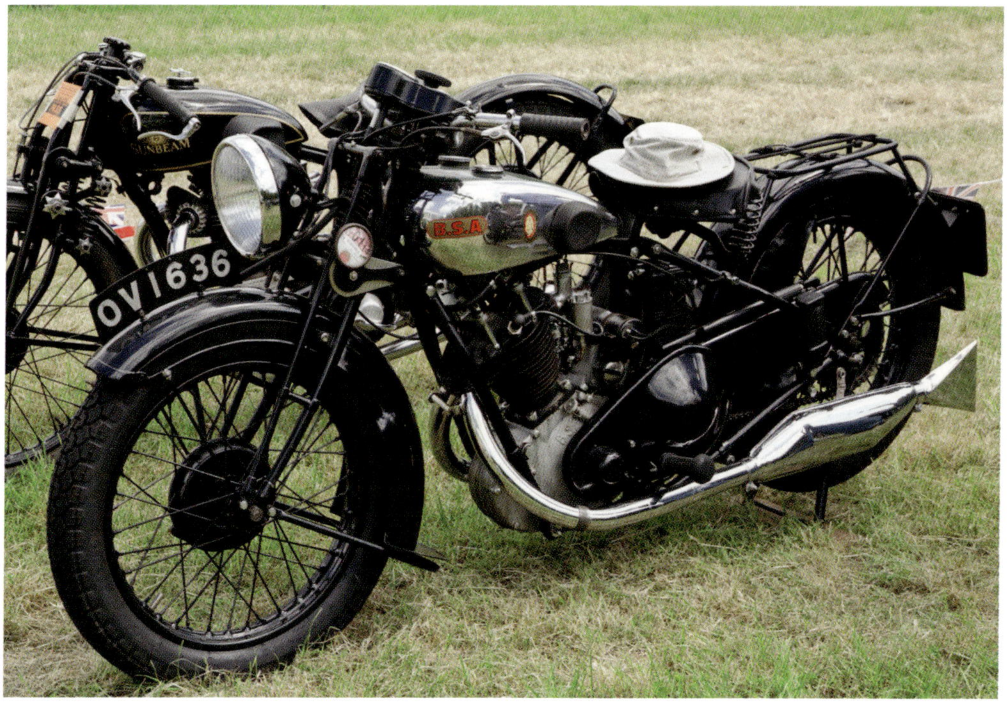

A 1931 BSA S31 Sloper. BSA would buy Sunbeam in 1943. SG2012

cooled; the new trend of placing 'saddle' fuel tanks above frame rails meant that, by moving the cylinder head forward, those frame rails could be lowered, and so in turn the saddle could be lowered; and thus the centre of gravity was lowered, improving road holding. Within a short time the Sloper – although never officially listed as such, despite BSA publicity using the name – started a trend that would see many of BSA's competitors adopt inclined motors.

The first models featured a 493cc engine and a single-port cylinder head, topped by a cast-aluminium cover for the rockers but with exposed valve springs. Alongside the cast-iron cylinder barrel were plated tubes to cover the pushrods. Gentle camshaft contours and wide bases on the tappets helped to achieve a quiet and smooth-running engine, and the large crankcase accommodated a big and heavy flywheel, to aid low speed torque and a steady ticko-

THE 'SLOPER' MODEL S

Year: 1928
Displacement: 493cc
Bore/stroke: 80 x 98mm
Engine type: Four-stroke overhea valve
Cylinders: 1
Weight: 162kg (357lb)
Top speed: 70–75mph (113–121km/h)

ver. With three speeds, wet-sump lubrication with separate, hand-operated metering, and offering good performance and handsome looks, the Sloper quickly established itself as a rider's favourite. There was also the option of a higher compression ratio and special cams for riders seeking more performance. 349cc and side-valve versions were offered from 1929 and, for 1930, chrome plate replaced nickel on all the brightwork, with a new, forged steel spine frame in place of the previous duplex layout.

The 493cc overhead-valve engines also gained a fashionable twin-port cylinder head with doubled-up exhausts and fishtail silencers. For 1930 BSA offered no fewer than eighteen models, six of which had inclined engines. By now there was an optional sporting kit for £10, including a high-compression piston, hardened valves and springs, and a racing sparkplug, but the company discovered there were few buyers. From 1932 all were equipped with a four-speed gearbox, but the Sloper range remained essentially vintage in character until its demise in 1935, by which time the line-up had shrunk to just two models: one overhead-valve, the other side-valve, both of 596cc.

CARS BETWEEN THE WARS

By the end of 1924 the bulk of BSA's profits came from cars and bicycles, and by 1930 these were the group's focus. BSA might have remained the largest manufacturer of motorcycles, but demand had halved and production was unprofitable, while BSA's cars – principally Daimlers – and bicycles now accounted for more than half of the group's turnover.

So as well as continuing the Daimler car range, BSA re-booted four-wheel production under their own banner in 1921 with a V-twin-powered 10HP 'light car'. This was no badge-engineered Daimler, but a genuine attempt to move into the light car market with an all-new, rear-wheel-drive model.

This car used an 85 x 90mm (bore x stroke) 1018cc V-twin engine based on the Hotchkiss-designed motor introduced in early 1921: we have already seen how Harold Briggs, late of Daimler, had taken inspiration from this French-designed motor when he penned the L28 and Sloper motorcycle engines. The rest of the new BSA car was certainly designed at Small Heath, although it was probably initially produced in one of BSA's other factories.

The car was eventually produced with V-twin 4- and 6-cylinder motors, the latter being a Knight sleeve valve engine. For 1923 the 4 was available rated at 11 and 12HP, and 14HP for 1924, which was the last year of production for both the 4 and V-twin models. From 1924 to 1926 a 6-cylinder 16HP version remained in production in a large, purpose-built factory on Coventry Road, known as the light car works. Yet production of these rear-wheel-drive cars never really amounted to much, with estimates of the total number produced at around 1,000 over four years. This was despite BSA's usual headline-grabbing publicity stunts, with the car challenging in many rallies during the twenties, doing well in the hands of Captain Brittain and Mr Danby. But strong competition from the cheaper Austin 7 forced a premature end to the light car, and so BSA ventured into front-wheel-drive three- and four-wheel cars for 1929.

It is only comparatively recently that front-wheel-drive cars have become popular, most famously with the Austin Mini in 1959, although it was not until the 1970s that the layout became commonplace. Although the idea of front-wheel drive arrived in the earliest days of motoring, manufacturers soon realized it was easier to build a car that steered with the front wheels and was powered from the rear. By the 1920s front-wheel-drive motoring was limited to relatively few models, notably the Alvis series one U1.

As BSA considered a return to the light car market, the three-wheel market then dominated by the Morgan caught their eye. Two wheels at the front was the popular configuration, and driving through a single rear wheel would allow motorcycle architecture, albeit with a heavy load on the single rear tyre. Front-wheel drive, on the other hand, offered an easily detachable rear wheel with no long and oily chain, ideas the sales team liked.

A BSA 10HP Roadster c. 1922–26, powered by a V-twin. BARNEY

A BSA front-wheel-drive three-wheeler powered by a 1021cc ohv V-twin. Production numbers reached around 5,200. CHARLES 01

So in November 1929 the BSA three-wheeler appeared, offering innovations such as a reverse gear, electric start and full weather protection. Independent front suspension was another benefit resulting from the front-wheel-drive layout, with *The Motor Cycle* reporting 'the details of this vehicle are of such interest that it may be said to mark a milestone in the history of the light runabout'. Indeed it did: this was the first mass-produced front-wheel-drive car, something that BSA would build on with their later four-wheelers, notably the Scout of 1935.

The new three-wheeler's engine was again based on the Hotchkiss V-twin, now configured as a 1021cc two-stroke, helping to stay within the 8cwt (406kg) taxation limit for three-wheelers. The engine was mounted with cylinders across the car and driving through a cork clutch and conventional gearbox to a differential mounted midway between the front wheels. Final drive was by shaft, with flexible fabric-based couplings and Hooke (universal) joints at the front wheels. Two coupled brakes were fitted, one on the rear wheel and one mounted to the right of the differential.

The first three-wheelers did not have any shock absorbers, but these were fitted to later models, apparently to prevent spring breakage. The suspension layout remained essentially the same throughout BSA's commitment to three- and four-wheelers, although later Scouts – the final BSA car – had outboard front drum brakes. Even the BSA/Daimler armoured car built during World War II had suspension of essentially the same design, albeit in a rather more substantial four-wheel-drive layout.

The 1930 BSA three-wheeler was available in sports or tourer guise, alongside a four-seater family model for 1931 that squeezed two small children's deckchair-style canvas seats in behind the main passenger seats. 1934 brought a commercial van version, but few were sold. Indeed it is surprising that BSA sold any three-wheelers, since they were only around 10 per cent cheaper than the £125 Austin 7, which offered four wheels, 4 cylinders, a steel roof and windows all round: this illustrates how expensive it seemed to tax a car rather than a three-wheeler, and how marginal most people's finances were.

In late 1931 BSA introduced a four-wheel version of the trike, dubbed the FW32 – front-wheel (drive) 1932 model – and also available as a two-seater, four-seater and van – but with higher tax to pay and no advantages other than road stability over the trikes, they found few buyers.

The 1933 three-wheelers were much improved, with a water-cooled 4-cylinder 9HP motor and refreshed bodywork that included new wings and longer bonnet. The three-wheelers would survive until 1936, but BSA had quickly realized they needed to design and build a proper car, one with four wheels and a proper roof. The fact that BSA had bought Britain's first car maker, Lanchester, in 1931 helped enormously.

So a more ambitious BSA car arrived in 1932, using the 9HP four to power either an open four-seat touring body (the T9) or as a van (the V9). But while the T9 proved pleasant enough, it was just too heavy, especially in the pricey automatic version with a fluid flywheel torque convertor, and only survived a year. Yet BSA remained determined to crack the car market.

BSA now backed both front- and rear-wheel-drive horses, 1932 also welcoming the Ten (HP) Saloon, which, although claimed to have been designed (and subsequently produced) at Small Heath, did have a remarkable similarity to the Lanchester Ten, with an 1185cc 4-cylinder motor and an automatic transmission borrowed from Daimler. It was an attempt to build a sizeable car at a lower price than the equivalent Lanchester, recognizing the effect of the Depression. The Ten was followed in 1934 by the 1378cc 6-cylinder BSA Light Six, again designed to be a lower cost version of the equivalent Lanchester.

Lanchester, manufacturers of the first motor car built on British soil in 1895, had been bought by BSA in 1931 when their upmarket client base was decimated by the Wall Street Crash, threatening to bankrupt the company. The name and what BSA took of the business was unceremoniously stuffed under Daimler's wing, BSA paying less than the assets of Lanchester alone were worth. Daimler would continue to produce Lanchesters into the 1950s, the firm also building armoured cars and munitions during World War II.

SCOUTING FOR CARS

But BSA's real efforts went into producing a successful four-wheel, front-wheel-drive car that culminated in the Scout, introduced in 1935. This was a two-seater with pleasing, if conventional, lines and a sporting bent. It used the three-wheeler T9 engine, a 1075cc 4-cylinder unit, with a three-speed (plus reverse) gearbox operated via a lever on the dashboard. The single differential brake at the front was the same as the three-wheeler, with drum brakes at the

BSA Scout Series 4, 4-cylinder, from October 1936. TONY HISGETT

rear operated by rods. Rear suspension was semi-elliptical springs. Chassis arrangements were similar to the T9.

The Scout sold well, and BSA was encouraged to produce a 10HP, 1204 cc version, the Series 2 (another two-seater) and the Series 3, in both four-seat open tourer and two-seat coupé form. By 1936 the potential BSA car buyer could choose between five front-wheel-drive models plus many more 'fluid flywheel' automatic, rear-wheel-drive, 4- and 6-cylinder saloons. The situation was rationalized during 1936 by culling the range, leaving just an improved Scout in two- and four-seat tourer and two-seat coupé bodies. These Series 4 Scouts featured an improved gear change and all-round drum brakes, rod and cable operated at the front. Later Scouts were fitted with a redesigned gearbox: although synchromesh could not be squeezed in, the straight-cut gears were replaced by offset double helical 'Silent Second' constant mesh sets.

For 1938 the Scout Series 5 upgraded the electrics from six to twelve volts, Bendix cable brakes and minor styling tweaks. For the final year of Scout production the 1939 Series 6 was fitted with 'easy clean' steel (rather than wire) wheels and a three-bearing crankshaft, now in two- and four-seat tourer bodywork, or as a saloon. Just before war broke out a two-seat drop-head coupé (convertible) version went into production, but only fourteen were built, and preparation for war brought BSA car production to a halt before the Series 7 got beyond the prototype stage.

In the end BSA produced some 6,650 three-wheelers between 1929 and 1935, and 3,000 Scouts of all types. With World War II looming, BSA car production ended, and with it died the world's first mass-produced front-wheel-drive car. Post-war BSA would leave the cars to Daimler and focus on motorcycles.

CHAPTER THREE

A RETURN TO MOTORCYCLES

In 1928 BSA's Redditch Eadie works closed, and all motorcycle production moved to Small Heath. The famous Bert Perigo also joined BSA's competition department, winning the inaugural British Experts Trial in 1929, the start of BSA's off-road superstar dynasty. But canny BSA didn't ignore the entry level models, appreciating that new riders often developed a loyalty to a marque when the time came to trade up. Many manufacturers achieved competitively priced entry level models by buying in Villiers' two-stroke motors, but that was never the BSA way. So for 1928 they designed their first and only two-stroke motorcycle (discounting the DKW-designed Bantam engine and the mopeds), a 175cc unit construction motor, although it would only last a few seasons.

In terms of its specification, the little BSA was a cut above the mostly Villiers-engined opposition, boasting a two-speed transmission, dry clutch and gear primary drive. The engine/gearbox unit was carried in a bolted-up duplex frame and there were two brakes, both of which operated on the rear wheel. Priced at £28 10s, the A28 comfortably undercut BSA's cheapest four-stroke model, the 249cc B28 De Luxe, which although good value compared to the opposition, cost a comparatively hefty £37 15s. The A28 could even be ordered with electric lights, albeit an expensive extra at the

A 1928 BSA Model A28 175 – the only BSA-designed two-stroke motorcycle. YESTERDAYS ANTIQUE MOTORCYCLES

A 1932 BSA W32-6 with sidecar. This was the basic 499cc side-valve version: the two new ohv equivalents were designated W32-7, while those with the tuned motors were listed as Blue Star, a name also applied to the equivalent 250 and 350 models. CRAIG HOWELL

time for such a basic commuter. The catalogue description was promising:

> *It's a machine that anyone can learn to ride in a few minutes, and ride with confidence, because it is so light, comfortable and easy to handle. The two-stroke engine is easy to start and very economical to run. This machine is fully capable of doing long distance journeys at a good average speed, and it is backed by the BSA reputation for consistent reliability.*

But the A28 didn't set BSA's tills ringing and, while cheap for a BSA, was costly compared to the Villiers or Blackburne-powered equivalents. BSA was associated with quality four-stroke singles, not two-stroke commuters: it needed to get back to its roots.

So in 1932 BSA's famous Star series was born, with the Blue Star ohv singles in 350 (3.49HP) and 500cc (4.99HP) capacities, designated L32-5 and W32-5 respectively. The 'Star' label indicated an improved specification over BSA's basic transport models, including a fashionable upswept twin pipe exhaust system. Inside the motor was a higher compression piston, stronger valve springs, racing camshaft and a spark plug fed by an Amal pump carburettor. There was the traditional BSA green petrol tank with an integral instrument panel and electric lighting. 1932 was also the year that BSA's famous combination levers were introduced, all models featuring details such as the clutch and magneto lever combined, as were the brake and air lever. Added to this, the Amal internal twist grips for throttle and ignition timing reduced significantly the juggling that riders had to do to maintain progress.

The Blue Stars also introduced the option of a foot- (rather than hand-) change gearbox, which was also available on three of the other singles, allowing BSA to claim a twenty-two strong 1932 range. A 250 (2.49hp) B33-3 Blue Star Junior joined the range for 1933, but without a foot-change option. All models now had electric lighting, with the acetylene option left to the history books. Such upgrades made BSA the world's leading producer of single-cylinder four-stroke motorcycles during the 1930s, despite the economic hardships that held sway for the much of that decade. Contrary to common belief the 1930s depression affected very specific groups, and many – perhaps even most in some parts of the country – people enjoyed a good and improving standard of living that made the coming war seem unthinkable. Surveys of the time showed that the vast majority believed Britain should disarm completely and spend the savings on reviving the areas of the country affected by recession. In the meantime they would go about their business on BSA's motorcycles, viewed as ruggedly dependable rather than innovative or sporting. The overhead-valve singles especially

LEFT: **A BSA 986cc Model G from the 1930s. As the publicity material ran: 'Both the de Luxe and Colonial machines have been expressly designed for Sidecar work with heavy loads. For high speeds or in difficult country the extra power given by the larger engine will add materially to the rider's comfort and the average road performance. The BSA 9.86HP twin-cylinder model is a typical example of the high standard of perfection to which the modern motor bicycle has been raised. As a super touring combination, it worthily upholds the highest traditions of British Engineering.'**

The riding position of the Model G offers tank top instrumentation.

The timing side of the side-valve 986cc Model G motor.

were coveted by countless young men who neither desired nor could afford a car.

Meanwhile the V-twin range carried on, albeit intermittently. For 1924 there had been 986cc 8HP versions, including a taxi and the range-topping Colonial. The following year the 750 returned to the fold and the 986 was upgraded to 9.86HP, bearing in mind that such ratings were based upon a tax calculation and that in today's terms this was likely to be over 30bhp – easily enough to exceed 100mph (160km/h). In 1929 the World Tour 1000 model was introduced, reflecting the return of the Colonial twins in 1928, which had done just that.

This was the inspiration for the 2012 travel book of the year *My Boy, Motor and I* edited by Marek Ponikowski, based on the chronicle of two fellow Poles. Stanislaw and Halina Korolec-Bujakowska bought a BSA V-twin in 1934, probably a G34-14 World Tour, to travel to China on a belated honeymoon. The young couple intended to finance the trip with news stories, including for *The World* and *Motorcycle*. They set out in August 1934 to reach Shanghai, China. In 1937, when Japanese bombs fell on Shanghai, Halina decided to return to Poland on the Trans-Siberian Railroad but Stanislaw stayed to serve with the RAF; the two were never reunited. The motorcycle probably just evaporated into war duties.

The gathering storm clouds in European politics may not have troubled many in Britain, but the War Department was not convinced by the calls for disarmament. At the 1933 Olympia show BSA had displayed a handsome newcomer in the form of a new, lightweight 498cc (63 × 80mm bore/stroke) ohv V-twin designated J34-11, often abbreviated to J11 or J34. The machine was not a new design, as it was based on a prototype commissioned by the War Office a year or so earlier. After extensive tests the military authorities were satisfied with its performance, and between 1933 and 1936 some 700 machines were apparently ordered, although others claim it was rejected altogether, the War Office tending to favour side-valve singles for military use.

All the author can say is that none seem to have been seen in khaki in public, despite the interest in military vehicles from this era, but that nine were delivered in April 1936 to the Royal Canadian Corps of Signals for despatch riders. 300 were also designated B15 by the RAF, sold not as part of a regular military contract, but rather privately to the War Office in June 1934. Apart from a BSA roundel on the top of the tank the bikes had no other markings or numbers, the military adding their own. These unmarked 'off the record' vehicles (including armoured cars) were destined for the Middle East. They were used in numerous ground combat operations by RAF Intelligence/6 Squadron during the Arab Revolt in what is now Palestine. However, it seems that repatriated military J11s were stamped as such if they were sold back into the civilian market, often with parts that the War Office had removed but which were reinstated with later fittings.

As to selling brand new into the civilian market, at £70 the J34 was 20 per cent more expensive than a comparable single but only slightly more powerful, so understandably, not many of these innovative machines were sold. This was despite these new models catching the public's imagination, and much favourable comment as the first overhead-valve – rather than side-valve – V-twins from BSA, which brought the twins into line with the more up-to-date singles. For 1935 few changes were made, but notably there was a new foot-change mechanism, redesigned front forks, and a speed-ometer on top of the front forks instead of in the tank panel.

So having appeared for the first time in civilian guise in the 1934, the '500' was joined by a 750 version, the Y13, before ceasing production at the end of 1936 as the J12. The Y13 was actually 748cc with a bore and stroke of 71 x 94.5mm and, although rated at 7.49HP for tax purposes, BSA claimed 26.5bhp at 4,800rpm, 4.5 more than for the 500. Featuring a four-speed gearbox, the Y13 continued until the end of the 1938 season, produced for only three years. The 748cc V-twin is today one of the rarest and most highly sought after of all 1930s BSAs, with only 1,600 built and far fewer surviving.

Meanwhile the 1000 V-twin was renamed the G14, the Small Heath publicists claiming that '...Police and other public services throughout the world have proved that this machine will give years of hard work with the minimum of attention and expense', while *Motor Cycling* magazine pressed the point that at £82 in 1938 with the mandatory speedometer an extra, the G14 was far from cheap, and few could afford such luxury. Even so, Jim Gaisford fell in love with the Y13 at the 1984 Lydiard Park Country Fair in north Wiltshire:

> *I was asking about the bike and the rider said 'I'm just about to ride in the show ring, so hop on the back and we can talk while I ride round'. So I said to my girl-friend 'give me half an hour', and we were off!' (Jim laughs, realizing how irrational this sounds.) Well, I was hooked and thought 'I've got to get me one of these'! So I did, but not even the horn worked on the one I bought, and it took five years to get anything else to work. They take a bit more energy to ride than the singles, but just do it, do it well, ride them hard, and they're awesome to ride.*

But what about the brakes, a notorious issue on compara-tively heavy motorcycles of the era?

> *I took it to a very clever engineer and basically chained it to his bench and said 'I'll unlock that when the brakes work'! He trued the drums, worked on the levers and put modern linings in. I'm not saying they're as good as modern brakes, but if you keep your eye on, say, the dog three cars ahead, you'll be fine.*

Jim Gaisford's BSA Y13.
STEVE SMITH

MODEL Y13

Year: 1934
Displacement: 748cc
Bore/Stroke: 71 x 94.5mm
Engine type: Four-stroke overhead-valve 50-degree V
Cylinders: 2
Weight: 204kg/450lb (wet)
Top speed: 90mph (145km/h)

A NEW START: VAL PAGE ARRIVES

Val Page, late of Ariel and Triumph, joined BSA in 1936. Page had left Ariel in 1932 to become chief designer at rivals Triumph, where, with Edward Turner, he developed Triumph's first parallel twin, the model 6/1, which was to presage the pre-war Tigers 70, 80 and 90. The concept of a parallel twin, familiar to us now but innovative at the time, would become the backbone of the post-war British motorcycle industry. But once installed at Triumph, Page discovered he couldn't get on with Turner, who in turn bore a grudge against BSA: the Triumph twin was effectively half of Turner's 1928 Square Four design that BSA had rejected and Ariel eventually picked up. The British motorcycle industry was always an incestuous business.

Settled in at BSA, Page revised and simplified models that had become uneconomic to produce, so making them profitable once more. He also designed all the new models (except the V-twins), including the Empire Star, which would be developed into the high performance production BSA Gold Star, named in celebration of Wal Handley's 100mph (160km/h) lap time at the Brooklands: the circuit gave a small gold star badge to any rider who lapped at 100mph or more. Handley had come out of retirement to ride a three-lap race for BSA at Brooklands, unusual in itself given that BSA had avoided road racing since the disastrous 1921 Senior TT when all their motorcycles had failed to finish. Winning the race with a fastest lap of 107.5mph (173km/h), Handley earned himself the gold star and with it launched the Gold Star marque.

BSA's stock rose on the back of Handley's performance on an apparently standard Empire Star with Page's new 499cc engine, not hurt by their reputation for excellent engineer-

BSA M23 Empire Star, and (behind) WM20 BSA RWD 10HP.

Civilian version of Val Page's M20.

ing and styling. The M23 Empire Star, available from 1936 in 250, 350 and 500 guises, sold well in the aftermath of Handley's win even though, at £70 for the bigger version, it was not cheap. This led to the first Gold Star, the M24 model. This had an aluminium alloy 496cc engine, a magnesium alloy gearbox, and a rigid frame made of light tubes without – perhaps a BSA big bike first – sidecar attachment lugs. This model continued up to the start of the war.

Page also designed the dependable BSA M20 motorcycle, with a 500 side-valve low compression engine and lots of low-end torque, which made it an ideal sidecar tug. When sent to the British Army for testing – without a sidecar – they didn't like it, considering it too heavy, slow, and with poor ground clearance. But it was saved by its toughness, reliability and ease of maintenance and repair. And of course, BSA was pretty much the world's largest motorcycle manufacturer, and also a huge defence contractor, which probably helped change hearts and minds. In the end, the army, the Royal Navy and the RAF placed huge orders for the M20, along with Sweden, South Africa and India. So, despite failing its initial test for military selection in 1936, later versions were revised and adopted by the army, and it saw action in many theatres of war.

MAUDES TROPHY PART II

In 1938 BSA won the Maudes Trophy for the second time, the coming tsunami of war briefly ignored in pursuit of publicity. A BSA M21 Combination and M23 Empire Star sharing duties for an ACU challenge of twenty climbs of Bwlch y Groes in Wales, then acceleration, speed and braking tests at Brooklands, followed by twenty more climbs of Bwlch y Groes. And then, for no obvious reason, crossing London in traffic, north-south and east-west, in top gear.

BSA's C range was also introduced in 1938, where a lightweight range was created by cannibalizing the physically larger B range, whose wheels and brakes were employed, the rest of the cycle parts a simple diamond hardtail frame and girder front fork. The BSA C11 was still pre-unit (that is, with separate gearbox and crankcase) with a single cylinder developed from the side-valve C10, both still with the 63 x 80mm bore and stroke of the 1924 Round Tank 250. Fitted with overhead valves and displacing 249cc, the C11 was launched in 1939 and continued to be developed into the 1950s, when it eventually gained plunger rear suspension.

Although British military only used a few C11s as light-

A 1947 BSA C10. Production ran from 1938 to 1957, with a moratorium for the war from 1942 to 1944.
70 MUSCLECAR RT+6

The C11 was the overhead-valve variant of the sidevalve C10 and a fellow time traveller until the unit C15 appeared in 1959.
PEPROVIRA

weight transport (having preferred the M20), in 1940 530 C11s were ordered in military specification by the Office of the High Commission of India. Modifications for war use included a rear carrier over the mudguard, an additional air filter on the fuel tank, and a magdyno in place of the coil.

BSA had now become the biggest motorcycle company in the world. By 1939, the company owned sixty-seven factories across the UK. During the war they made so much more than motorcycles but, despite this being the story of BSA motorcycles, more than a little of it will be told here.

CHAPTER FOUR

A WORLD AT WAR

As the clouds of war gathered once more, BSA were far more prepared than they had been in 1914. This initiative started amongst the visitors to the 1935 Leipzig fair, which included two executives from BSA, the senior being James Leek. Upon his return to Small Heath, Leek warned the directors that war was inevitable and, despite the lack of government backing since 1918, the board courageously sanctioned Leek's request for extra cash to allow BSA to resume its role as a private arms manufacturer. When war was declared, BSA's planning office and tool room had been on overtime for three years.

Bernard Docker might have been chairman of BSA at the time, but he was also chairman of Midland Bank. In practice most decisions were made by Leek as the new managing

Armourers install .303 Browning machine guns into the rear turret of an Armstrong Whitworth Whitley Mk V of 58 Squadron RAF at Linton-on-Ouse, Yorkshire, in June 1940.
ROYAL AIR FORCE

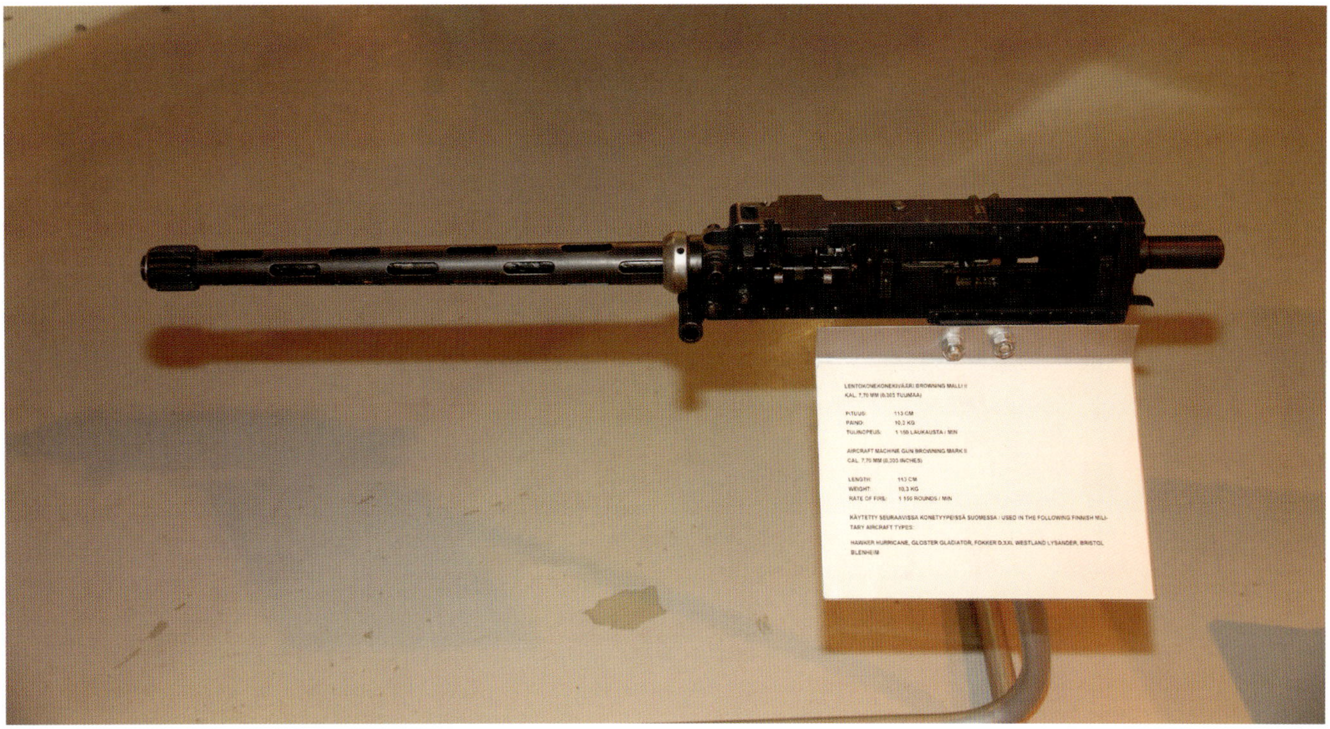

A .303 Browning Mk II aircraft machine gun. MKFI

director: he had taken up the role in 1937, after which he returned to Germany on a fact-finding mission. He came home to warn the government that he had seen 'the bullets [that] were for England'.

Leek wasn't alone in preparing for rearmament. From 1935 the government had started the 'shadow' factory scheme, which hints at secrecy but was nothing of the sort. The Luftwaffe's General Erhard Milch was paid a consultancy fee for advice on shadow factories in Birmingham and Coventry in late 1937. 'Back-up' factories might have been a better term, as the new facilities were intended to offer an alternative to the main factories – especially for aircraft production – should these have to cease production following attack. Naturally they were camouflaged as soon as war was declared, and were part of the reason BSA grew to control sixty-seven factories. These would include units at Tipton, Dudley, Smethwick, Blackheath, Lye, Kidderminster, Stourport, Tyseley and Bromsgrove to assemble Browning machine guns; Stoke, Corsham and Newcastle-under-Lyme to build Hispano cannons; and Leicester and Studley Road to produce the Besa machine gun. Ruislip built the Oerlikon 20mm cannon, Stafford rocket projectiles, Tamworth two-pound gun carriages, Mansfield the Boys anti-tank gun and Shirley produced rifles. BSA products were also manufactured by other companies under licence.

This period running up to World War II is often portrayed as one of naive appeasement just waiting for Winston Churchill to grasp the levers of power and belatedly prepare Britain for the conflict to come. But in truth prime minister Stanley Baldwin had been trying to rearm the country, and he believed that this cost him the 1937 general election. In the Peace Ballot of 1935 over 10 million British voters petitioned for disarmament, as opposed to fewer than 900,000 who were against the idea. People wanted any available money to be spent on the aftermath of the Depression, and most believed Britain could sit out the Nazis' takeover of continental Europe, Switzerland style.

This was the real naivety that tied the hands of politicians such as Baldwin, with Hitler already demanding designs for bombers that could reach Washington from Europe, and with Britain earmarked as George Orwell's 'Airstrip One', or at least feared as a base that could disrupt missions from France. Fortunately people such as Leek saw the inevitable and, along with the workers at 'The BSA', prepared for war through gritted teeth. Leek

ABOVE: **A BSA M20 in a display of military vehicles.**

Detail of an M20 – note the 'blackout' headlight cover.

disregarded the government's orders and production guidelines, and set about making as much as the factory could possibly build. 'Everything from barbed wire up, really', as one worker remembered when asked what they had made during the war.

How quickly things changed is perfectly illustrated by Pat Slinn's tale of his father telling him how the stockpile of civilian motorcycles was unceremoniously repurposed for the Army: 'Rubber mats were put over the seat and the engine roughly masked. They were then sprayed matt khaki, with overspray everywhere and the original paintwork still visible under places like the seat. It was done in a hurry.' BSA, like everyone else in Britain, had to get on a war footing without delay or ceremony.

Once the humiliation of Dunkirk made an attempt to invade southern England a racing certainty, there was an acceptance that a Nazi invasion force had to be held back long enough to re-equip the army. Dunkirk, while a heroic operation to rescue men, also cost the British most of their equipment. Everything from tanks to bicycles was abandoned, along with many BSA motorcycles and weapons. BSA went to twenty-four-hour shifts, seven days a week, with 100-plus hour working weeks commonplace. Hilda Hogg, one of many women who worked those hours, remembers dances at lunchtimes and variety shows in the evenings: 'We made our own happiness, we had to – otherwise it'd get you down 'cause all we did was work.' Except for most of the women, once they'd clocked off there was family to care for and loved ones to write to.

The first and perhaps most important beneficiary of Leek's prescience was the RAF in the run-up to the Battle of Britain. Lord Beaverbrook had been charged by Churchill with equipping the RAF, and Beaverbrook's stroke of genius was rationalization. Unlike the Luftwaffe, which chased the perfect aircraft for each job, Beaverbrook insisted on limiting alternatives: the RAF was to be supplied with just two fighters, the Hurricane and the Spitfire. Moreover these would share engines and weapons: the Rolls-Royce Merlin and the Browning .303 machine gun.

The same was true of the rest of the RAF's fleet, meaning efficient mass production and aircraft that could be fixed and rearmed if they landed away from their home airfield. During the war BSA produced more than 5 billion munitions components, including 468,098 Browning guns and 10 million shell fuses: this amounted to 1,650 pieces every minute, day and night, throughout the war.

An armourer of No. 3101 Servicing Echelon uses a periscope unit to adjust one of the .303 Browning machine guns on a Supermarine Spitfire Mark IXB of No. 341 (Free French) Squadron RAF, jacked up before a gun harmonization board at Biggin Hill, Kent. IMPERIAL WAR MUSEUMS. PILOT OFFICER MILLER, RAF PHOTOGRAPHER

Early (1941) Supermarine Spitfire with eight .303 Browning machine guns. These were always covered by tape (red here) on take-off to minimize air resistance. ALAN WILSON

UNREPORTED TRAGEDY AFTER A BOMBING RAID

That those Brownings were churned out by BSA in numbers far greater than was originally imagined was to Britain's great fortune during the Battle of Britain, with one BSA employee pointing out that 'without guns a Spitfire's just a pretty thing'. Which is why the Luftwaffe needed to destroy BSA and, early in the evening of 19 November 1940, set about doing just that, following the canals that would guide Nazi explosives to BSA's factories. Even in the dark the low-flying bombers' markings could be seen by locals heading to air-raid shelters. But not by the BSA's night-shift workers.

BSA's evacuation plan involved heading across a bridge over the canal to a purpose-built shelter, but most employees feared they'd be caught in the open. Instead they would head to the factory's basement, unaware that on this occasion they were making a fatal mistake. Two bombs scored a direct hit on one of the most modern factory buildings, its floor collapsing into the basement along with all the factory's machinery. The result was the biggest single loss of life in a British factory during the war, with fifty-three killed and eighty-nine injured. Many were women, or those too young or too old to fight. It was six weeks before the final body was recovered.

Yet nothing was reported beyond 'bombs fell on a West Midlands town', because a government 'D' notice prohibited it, and would continue to do so for thirty years. Birmingham was too important a manufacturing centre to let anybody know that it had been critically wounded. So while the story of Coventry's horror is well known, Birmingham's is not, despite the fact that it received twice the tonnage of Nazi bombs as its near neighbour and 1,000 more fatalities. Indeed, only London was bombed more.

In the unreported horror came heroism. Two electricians working on the fatal night shift were recognized for saving lives that would have otherwise been lost. Alf Stevens grabbed an oxy-acetylene cutter and set about the girders trapping his workmates. One man he rescued returned home only to find that that, too, had been bombed: fortunately his wife was visiting a neighbour, and was safe. Stevens was assisted by Alf Godwin, who was awarded the Empire Medal for his efforts, while Stevens received the George Medal, Britain's second highest civilian award.

BSA'S WORLD WAR II TWO-WHEELERS

In 1941 BSA was approached to produce a new pedal cycle with a maximum weight of just 22lb (about 10kg) especially for airborne use, a figure that BSA's final offering comfortably undercut. Over 60,000 of these folding bicycles were produced, half the total production of military bicycles during the war, yet they are often forgotten. 'Dropping tests' from aircraft by parachute were undertaken in 1942 for the 'Second Pattern Airborne' folding paratrooper's bicycle, with sliding peg pedals to make them easier and safer to land alongside. Folded by releasing two wingnuts on the curved top and down tubes, the bicycle would be attached to a rope so that it landed just before its rider. A bracket allowed a Lee Enfield rifle to be stowed alongside the downtube, and some had front lights that could be attached to a belt and so used away from the bicycle.

The Airborne was used, but not as much as originally intended. The British Airborne Forces used a few on operations, but as larger vehicles such as the Jeep were available by June 1944, transported in by gliders, the bicycles became less important. Some were probably used on the first airborne raid into Norway, as they were found in the wreckage of the gliders. Ironically, when the airborne division did use bicycles in great numbers, on the advance to Wismar in Germany in 1945, they used stolen ones.

On D-Day, 6 June 1944, each Commando unit was listed as having a bicycle platoon, but it seems the bicycles were quickly abandoned. Ironically the greatest use of the BSA airborne bicycle in action was by British and Canadian infantry during the invasion of Normandy. Some were also used for the invasion of Sicily in 1943 by Canadian infantry. Post war some were retrofitted with the 1950s Cyclemaster engine, developed by DKW during the war, and made post war in EMI factories in Hayes, Middlesex, as part of war reparations; BSA would build the BSA Bantam on the same basis.

The usual mix of production featured in BSA's 1939 motorcycle production (*see* Appendix) and, while from much of 1941 until the end of the war BSA's motorcycle output was entirely War Department M20s, initially this mix remained. B29 350 Silver Sports were produced in 1940, alongside more prosaic W (for War Department) B30s. An original contract was for fifty of these 350s, supplied to the British Army in 1941, but further contracts were abandoned in favour of the even more prosaic M20, probably forced by tooling availability and some reliability issues around the B30.

A 350 C12 was also built in 1940 and 1941, a model name that wouldn't reappear until 1956, by which time it

A BSA Second Pattern Airborne folding paratrooper's bicycle circa 1940. SCIENCE MUSEUM CCL

BSA tried to make sure people knew who had made their kit, even in war. BIRMINGHAM MUSEUMS TRUST

A 1953 BSA Winged Wheelby, often fitted retrospectively to BSA's wartime bicycles. STEVE GLOVER

was a four-speed 250 in a more modern frame as a C11 update. 1940 also saw the final production run for the G14 V-twin.

THE WM20 – THE MOTORCYCLE THAT WON THE WAR?

As we have seen, the BSA M20 was designed by Val Page, plugging a gap in BSA's range for an economical sidecar tug. To this end it retained a hand gear change and a low frame, which compromised ground clearance off road but helped to maintain stability and a low seat height. Although the bottom end was similar across the BSA range of singles, the M20 featured heavyweight flywheels and a low compression ratio which allowed it to pull away from a standstill in almost any gear and, once into the top of its four gears, to potter along at an acceptable pace regardless of the weight of a sidecar and its contents. The brakes were very good for the time, and although BSA's side-valve motors were slow, could run hot and, also used more fuel than most, they were very reliable and could run on poor quality fuel.

But as we have seen, the war department wasn't impressed with the M20 for all these reasons, and even BSA accepted the failings. The M20 was a sidecar tug, after all, although there was also the M21 with more capacity and even heavier flywheels if you were certain the motorcycle would spend its entire life as part of an outfit. Initially with a bore and stroke of 85 x 105mm to give 596cc, from 1938 the M21 shrank to 592cc by adopting the M20's 82mm bore and a 112mm stroke. The last wartime M21s were built in 1940, although it would be resurrected for peacetime duties.

BSA had already sold the War Department B29 singles, but they were mainly lost in France post Dunkirk. BSA then created what it thought the military wanted: the ohv 348cc B30 single, which would work well in conditions similar to the environment around the trenches of World War I, which is how people initially expected World War II to play out. Fifty pre-production bikes were submitted for trials with much weight saving, and even the hairpin valve springs and alternator lighting of the original design. The hairpin valve springs were soon deleted following high rates of valve guide wear, and replaced by conventional springs. Nonetheless the War Department had been impressed with the B30 and ordered 10,000 of them, with the final ones built in 1941. But from this point on, presumably due to reliability issues

A BSA G14 with sidecar and machine gun.
ALF VAN BEEM

A BSA M20 in full wartime regalia.

around the lightweight and comparatively complex B30, it was M20s all the way. Plus BSA was geared up to build them in their thousands.

In truth the M20's big advantage was almost certainly that it was available. During the initial tests it had been in competition with machines from Matchless, Norton, Triumph and Royal Enfield. But BSA had been gearing up for war as early as 1935, well before the government asked them to. So, while the military preferred the Matchless G3L single and a side-valve twin from Triumph, Matchless couldn't promise the number of machines required, and Triumph's drawings, prototypes and tooling were destroyed in a bombing raid.

BSA alone was tooled up and ready to build the numbers the military needed. The WM20 would become the longest-serving motorcycle in British military history, and the one most supplied to the War Department.

The War Department specification included a large 8in (about 20cm) headlight, complete with the civilian model's switch panel and ammeter. The timing side cover – that is, the side that drives the camshaft and so valve timing – had a threaded plug allowing access to the magneto drive nut. There were flip-up (rather than screw-on) filler caps for both petrol and oil tanks, since these were things you didn't want to lose. There was a partially rod-operated front brake, and a speedometer drive from the front wheel rather than the more usual rear wheel fitting. BSA added a superfluous but cannily branded alloy tappet cover with their piled rifles emblem. Although by 1941 the alloy had to give way to steel, the logo remained. The cylinder-head stay and pillion facilities were also deleted. Some models also had an oil-pressure warning poppet on the timing cover, and there was an additional long stand at the rear on the left to supplement the wheel stands.

Even after the war had started a few M20 models were pencilled in for customers in Sweden, South Africa and India, according to the factory records. Even by spring 1940 BSA was still exporting, including to the Netherlands, Ireland, India and South Africa, as well as supplying UK dealers.

In 1939 there was a smaller 3 gallon (about 14ltr) fuel tank and revised girder forks, along with narrow mudguards less prone to clogging with mud, and service experience driving changes. In North Africa, where roads didn't really exist, riders wanted readily adjustable front dampers, the first in 1941 being a Bakelite knob, and later pressed steel. The headlight was changed to a 6in item with a hooded, slotted black-out cover, and a universal War Department tail light.

By early 1942 there was a rear carrier and sump guard, and pillion facilities were reinstated: lower ranking officers could now be given a lift rather than using increasingly scarce staff cars. Also scarce was rubber following Japan's invasion of Malaysia, so in late 1942 the WM20 lost all rubber fittings, and handlebar grips were simply canvas. But still BSA plugged away at getting WM20s built and, once in the field, the WM20s also kept plugging away. It would be the end of the war and 1945 before BSA built any other type of motorcycle, and the M20 would remain in production until 1956. Its long-stroke sibling, the M21, went even further, surviving until 1963.

Insomuch as anybody could, BSA had a good war. Production was maintained despite bombing, repeatedly at the Lanchester and Daimler Radford works in Coventry, which, ironically, probably built the Daimler Scout (aka Dingo) that Field Marshal Rommel used to escape in after his defeat at El Alamein. As the war ended, financially the BSA group was in good shape. It bought the Sunbeam motorcycles and bicycle business from Associated Motor Cycles in 1943, and then Ariel in 1944, when BSA chiefs moved Val Page back to his old home. If anybody was ready for the post-war world, it was BSA.

BSA ended 1944 with two priceless assets: domination of the world's motorcycle market, and a devoted workforce at Small Heath. Yet those in charge little appreciated the latter especially, having been too often appointed by the 'old boys' network',

A Daimler Dingo Scout, similar to the one Rommel used to escape in. A BSA design, built by Daimler from 1939 to 1945, with a 2.5-litre 6-cylinder 55bhp engine. 6,626 were produced.

CARCHRISNYE

Another M20 at a country fair, a reminder of less happy times.

where being able to fit in at the top of society and, ideally, to read a balance sheet, was considered enough. A knowledge of motorcycles or even engineering was considered unnecessary, which was in striking contrast to, say, Japan or Germany where at least some science qualifications were considered essential if you were to rise to the top of a manufacturing business. In his 1981 book, *Whatever Happened to the British Motor Cycle Industry?* designer Bert Hopwood wrote:

> *The war years demonstrated that BSA had a deep reserve of good will and technical and administrative skill at its disposal. The tragedy of peace was that this reserve was never properly harnessed, and good men eventually became disillusioned with what they perceived to be the incompetence of the company's directors and senior managers, many of whom had been brought in from outside and had little or no understanding of its products.*

A storm was coming, and captains of industry who had managed magnificently on the canal boats of Birmingham were about to discover if they had the mettle to change direction on a super tanker far out at sea.

THE M20

Year: 1937
Displacement: 496cc
Bore/stroke: 82 x 94mm
Compression ratio: 5:1
Engine type: Four-stroke side-valve vertical single
Carburation: Amal
Ignition system: Lucas 6V magneto dyno
Claimed power: 13bhp at 4,200rpm
Transmission: Multi-plate wet clutch, four-speed gearbox
Brakes: 7in single leading shoe front and rear
Wheels: 19in; 3.25in front, 3.50in rear
Weight: 167kg (369lb)
Top speed: 50mph (80km/h)

CHAPTER FIVE

EXPORT OR DIE – THE BIG TWINS

Britain's trade deficit – the gap between the value of what was exported and what was imported – had been growing since the mid-1930s, and World War II effectively brought overseas sales to an end, while the country imported everything from food to fighter aircraft. In 1941 Britain and the United States signed the Atlantic Charter, expressing the ideal of free trade yet, by the end of the war, Britain had lost two-thirds of its export markets and was having to rely upon American loans as well as repaying the wartime lease-lend arrangements. With the Empire fading fast there was really only one market to look towards – the United States itself.

Furthermore, nationalization meant that British steel production was under government control, a government that, from 1947, insisted that steel would only be available to businesses which exported at least 75 per cent of their production. How strictly this was applied is a moot point,

Early A7 plunger frame. Note the tiny front brake.

A 1947 A7 with a rigid frame. The motorcycle behind is the final version of Honda's 500 Four, the mid-seventies CB550F2: it produced 50bhp at 8,500rpm, compared to 35bhp at 4,500 for the A7. STEVE GLOVER

but the message was simple: export or die. And while BSA could rapidly put their singles back into production, perhaps tweaked as off-roaders for the huge demand in the United States, what they really needed was a big twin to compete with Harley-Davidson's offerings.

The American market wasn't hard to understand. Big distances meant big twin-cylinder engines, and grid layouts in towns and cities meant traffic lights. Traffic lights meant a chance to accelerate away quickly from a standing start, which also meant big engines, but in a motorcycle as light as possible so that energy went into moving forwards rather than moving mass. Americans returning from war were already showing the way, buying ex-military Harleys and taking everything off them that wasn't necessary, including cutting rear mudguards as short as possible – 'bobbing' as it became known.

Edward Turner, Triumph's chief designer and managing director, had launched just what was wanted at the 1937 National Motorcycle Show with the Speed Twin: an overhead valve, 498cc twin in a lightweight frame and the first truly successful British parallel twin, setting the template for many more to follow. Turner's twin was a major turning point for the British motorcycle industry, despite hardly being revolutionary. The 5T Speed Twin model was lighter than many contemporary singles with significantly more power and torque. 28bhp at 6,300rpm sounds relatively unimpressive today, but it was significantly more than any 500 single and weighed less than most of them as well. BSA needed an equivalent, realizing it as soon as the Speed Twin was shown.

The A7 was BSA's answer, initially sketched out by Val Page before passing the task for completion to Herbert Parker

– 'a first class engineer' according to Bert Hopwood – and David Munro, to create the first of the BSA twin-cylinder motorcycles since the V-twins. The outbreak of World War II delayed the launch, although several prototypes were built despite hostilities, reputedly with input from Norton race guru Joe Craig and even Edward Turner. A prototype A7 was flown to Paris for the first motorcycle show after the end of the war in September 1946, with production starting the following year. People must have looked at this brave new world and considered BSA's bicycle factory's strapline: 'It's time you had a BSA!' Oddly BSA chose instead to market its motorcycles with the strapline: 'Leave it to your BSA!'

The 495cc parallel twin – a first for BSA, marketed as a vertical twin – apparently produced 26bhp at 6,000rpm, making it capable of 82mph (132km/h); however, no claims as such were made in advertising material, even if 'fastest in class' certainly was, despite most agreeing that the Triumph Speed Twin was quicker. *The Motor Cycle* called the A7 'an outstandingly attractive machine... assured of a brilliant future'. The bore and stroke of 62 x 82mm was different to BSA's 250's 63 x 80mm, proving it was an all-new design, although the recessed nine studs that fastened the cast-iron cylinder head needed well-made box spanners or the then rare sockets. As with other British motorcycles of the period, this was asking for oil leaks, especially once worked on away from the factory, and the situation was not helped by the retention of horizontally split crankcases. But to improve oil tightness as well as handling and convenience, the A7 featured a new engine and gearbox layout, dubbed 'semi-unit' by BSA. Here the crankcase and the gearbox were bolted to one another, with the gearbox in a fixed position.

Primary chain adjustment was accomplished with a slipper-type tensioner inside the chain case, rather than by moving the gearbox relative to the crankcases – and embarking on a juggling act to get both primary and final drive chain tension correct. The 'semi-unit' design not only made chain adjustment much easier, but also made for a much more rigid engine/gearbox structure, almost on a par with 'unit construction' types, where the gearbox and crankcase comprised one unit. The A7's gearbox was also all new, with four speeds foot shifting that was lighter, more compact and nicer to use than the units on BSA's singles.

The power unit included cast-iron cylinders and head, which BSA called monobloc: it was intended to provide excellent air flow to hot spots, with large openings between the cylinders and below the rocker boxes. The widely splayed exhaust ports and the rear pushrod tunnel also helped, as well as looking good. Aluminium alloy crankcases, with the cam behind the cylinder block, had 360-degree crank pins providing one power stroke for every engine revolution, with the pistons rising and falling together. The silicone alloy pistons were flat-topped with a compression ratio of 6:1, to accommodate the low-octane 'pool' petrol available in Europe at the time, drawn in by a single Amal carburettor.

From 1949 a sports version was available, dubbed the Star Twin. This had twin carburettors and plunger suspension as standard, with matt silver paint and chrome; yet Star Twin's top speed was barely higher than the original A7, topping out at 84mph (135km/h).

Located in a duplex frame with a rigid rear end, and BSA's telescopic forks (which made their debut in 1945 on the B31), the result was 'a dependable workhorse for everyday use... a machine that could be serviced in a back yard with just a few basic tools' according to author Owen Wright. BSA's first 'plunger' rear suspension was shown at the 1948 Earls Court Motorcycle Show, and production began with the 1949 top-of-the-range A7, the Star Twin. The plunger frame would be adopted into the entire 500 twin line-up for the 1950 model year.

While the plunger improved comfort over a rigid frame, handling suffered. The plunger was widely used by motorcycle manufacturers at the time for the same reason that BSA chose it: it allowed them to continue with their old rigid frames with few modifications, rather than ditching them for an entirely new swing-arm frame. But Norton's Featherbed frame was proving that change was inevitable and, as we shall see, BSA was already experimenting with a swing arm by 1948.

So the A7 looked the part, was reasonably priced at £171 10s, and it went well. It might not have had the glamour and pace of the Triumph Speed Twin, but it was quieter and came with BSA's reputation for quality and reliability. As the BSA owners' club advises: 'These machines were not the most sprightly or attractive of the vertical twins, but were certainly the most hard wearing, oil tight and the quietest, running with a minimum of whine or clatter.'

Mindful of this, in May 1948 Bert Hopwood arrived at BSA charged with refreshing the twin-cylinder models, averring in an interview that 'I was asked to redesign the 500cc twin engine to permit unimpeded air cooling and a more efficient combustion function. At the same time a 650cc version was designed, which became the Golden Flash.'

A fine illustration in a BSA advertisement showing off the later one-piece rocker cover.

BELOW: A wonderful Golden Flash spotted on the Isle of Man. Note the early Rocket III behind.

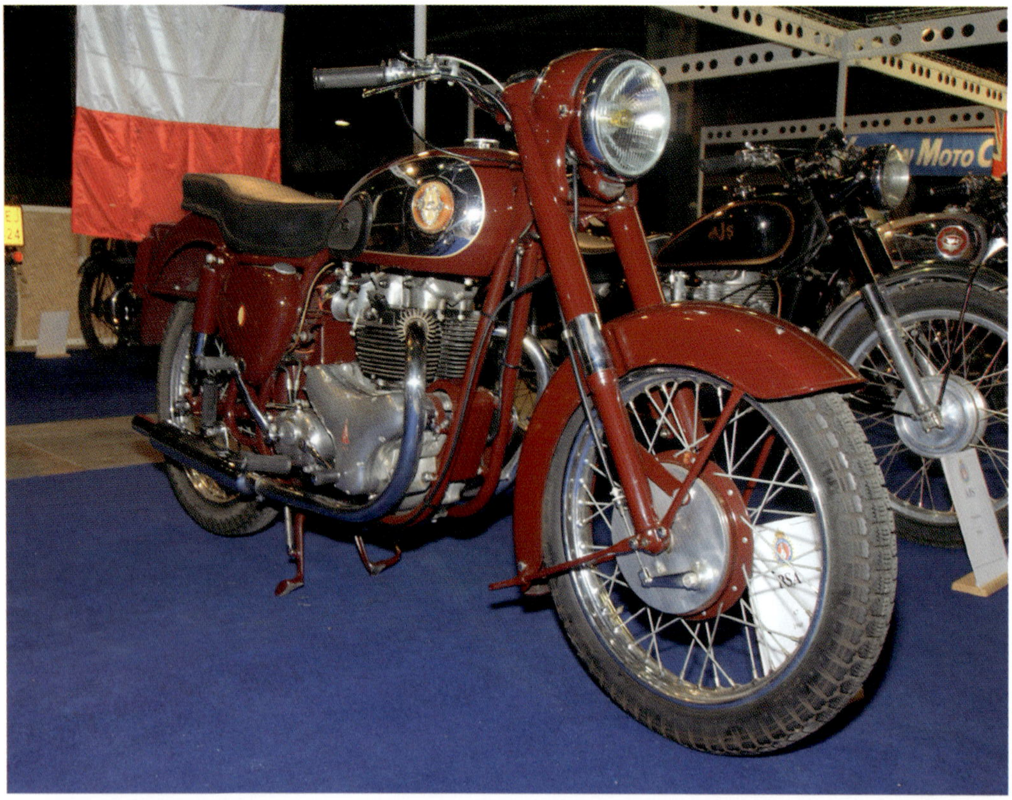

A 1960 A7. ALF VAN BEEM

BELOW: **Gold Flash advertisement.**

Hopwood had gone straight from school to work at Ariel under Val Page. Following Ariel's acquisition of a struggling Triumph in 1936, Hopwood was moved there under Edward Turner, then working on the Speed Twin. A growing reputation led to a job offer from Norton in April 1947 before the move to BSA. Clearly Hopwood had become the man to ask about vertical twins, and BSA needed an answer to Triumph's 650 Thunderbird that was targeted at the US market – and would score a bullseye.

Unlike Triumph, whose 650 was a bored and stroked 500, BSA started afresh with their 650, which only referenced the 500 A7 as a starting point, which would speed up getting the model into production. Even so, Hopwood's 650 – its full name the A10 Golden Flash – predictably followed the A7's architecture, aiming to improve performance without affecting reliability or introducing teething problems. So, like the 500 A7, the new 650 A10 had vertically split aluminium alloy crankcases with a semi-unit four-speed gearbox.

But even if externally the A10 engine looked similar to the original A7's – and they did share some components – almost everything was different. Hopwood, aided by David Munro, made the A7's 62 x 82mm bore and stroke much squarer at 70 x 84mm to give 646cc: clearly they were chasing power rather than torque, and customers who wanted a sporting solo rather than a sidecar lugger. The bore spacing was wider than the old A7's, making the crank longer and requiring more substantial crankcases. The one-piece forged steel crank benefitted from BSA's advanced metals division, with rod journals specified as 'induction-hardened, ground and polished'. Conrods were lightweight RR56 aluminium alloy.

And while the A7 soldiered on with an iron cylinder head, the A10 had an all-new lightweight aluminium alloy head with a shallower valve angle, reworked finning for better cooling, and a single rocker box instead of two. This is probably the easiest way to differentiate the models, and indeed an early

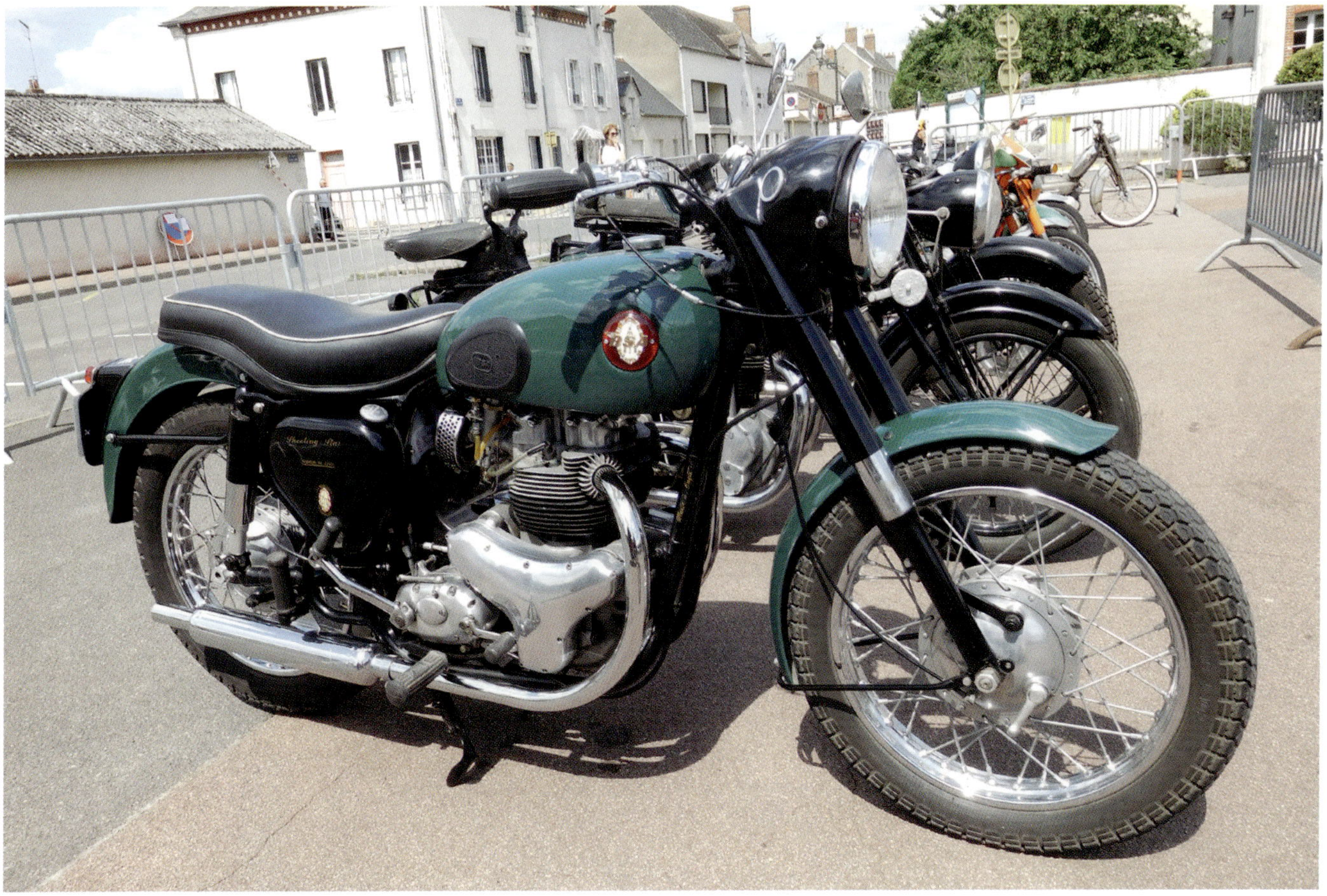

A 1964 BSA A7 Shooting Star.

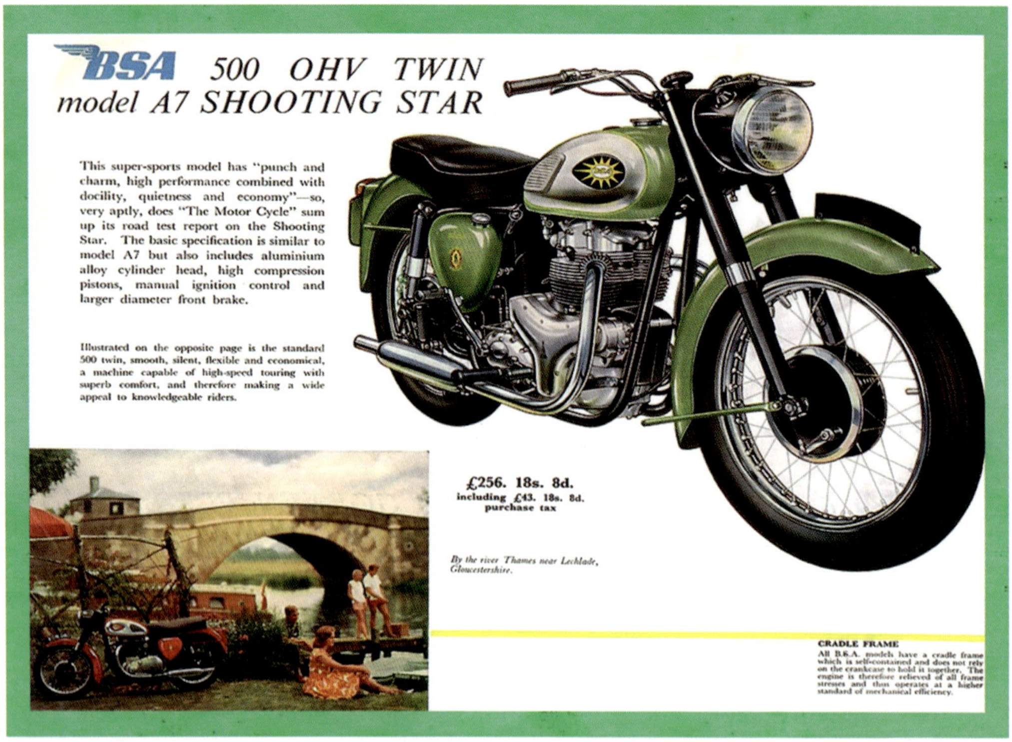

Advertisement for a late A7 Shooting Star.

A7 from a later version. An early A7 will have two rocker boxes, but later models and the A10 have a single, larger one. The A10's cylinder head also had an integral intake manifold (rather than bolt-on) for its single Amal carburettor.

First on sale in 1950, the A10 carried BSA's new 8in (up from 7in on the A7) single leading shoe (SLS) front brake. But the frame was the same as the A7's, and the A10 was available with either a rigid or plunger frame, the former probably handling better, especially as the plungers wore. A new swing-arm frame wouldn't arrive until 1954. Front suspension was via telescopic forks with hydraulic damping, while most everything else was carried over from the A7, and so proved robust and reliable, as was expected from BSA.

From its launch the A10 was available in very distinctive gold and chrome tinware with red pin striping, which might have reflected the Golden Flash's name had BSA not advertised the colour as beige. However, the standard colour scheme was black and chrome to appeal to BSA's traditionally conservative buyers. But advertisements in US magazines used the extrovert's colour scheme with straplines, including 'A 40 cubic inch spring-frame challenger built from the crankcase up'. Clearly what BSA was challenging was Triumph's success. The advertisement's boasts also included: 'Designed for American riders! Engineered for high speed! Constructed for rugged going!'

It was a powerful machine for its day, with 100mph (160km/h) potential, and could run the quarter mile in 16 seconds – a pedestrian time more associated with a 250's performance today, but impressive in 1951. There were grumbles that the 100mph (160km/h) press bikes had been specially prepared to make sure they were at least as fast as – and ideally faster than – the Triumph Thunderbird. So successful was the machine that in 1951 the A10 outsold the Triumph 650 Thunderbird.

With the A10 650 established, a revised A7 was launched in 1951, the new 500 engine sharing very few components with its predecessor. Instead the A10 and the redesigned A7 were extremely similar under the skin, with most parts interchangeable. The new A7 had a much shorter stroke than its forerunner, reduced by nearly 10mm, which gave a slightly different capacity of 497cc and a livelier feel to the motor: specifically from 1951 the first A7's 62 x 82mm 495cc became 66 x 72.6mm and 497cc. The bigger bore allowed shallower combustion chambers, and in turn a narrower valve angle, matching the A10's layout. Compression ratio rose to 6.7:1, with an option of 7.2:1, indicative of the improving fuel quality in Britain. There wasn't a great deal of difference in the ultimate power produced by the new motor however, up just 2bhp to 28bhp at 6,300rpm, but it would rev a little higher and with a little more vigour.

In 1954 when the swinging arm was introduced, the A7 and A10 reverted to the previous separate gearbox. Electric power came via two independent systems (the norm for bigger British motorcycles of the era): the reliable and self-contained Lucas magneto that allowed the engine to run without a battery, plus a dynamo generator to charge the battery and provide lights. Carburation was initially a single Amal remote float Type 6 – later an Amal TT, and then 376 Monoblocs were fitted.

ANOTHER MAUDES TROPHY

The strapline 'constructed for rugged going' was something BSA was keen to prove, and they set out for a third stab at winning the Maudes Trophy with the revised A7 Star Twin. The audacious plan was to take three standard bikes and three riders, under ACU observation, ride to Austria and compete in the era's most challenging branch of motorcycle sport: the 1952 International Six Days Trial (ISDT – renamed International Six Days Enduro by the FIM in 1981). The riders would then travel north through Germany, Denmark and Sweden to Oslo in Norway. There would then be a speed test before the saddle-sore riders returned, still aboard the A7s, to Birmingham.

One of the Maudes Trophy-winning A7s in the UK's National Motorcycle Museum.

The ISDT – an event Steve McQueen would come to relish – was to be held in the high lakes and mountain districts of Salzburg for 1952. That BSA was convinced their ambitious plan could win the Maudes Trophy was less risky than it might appear. They had Bert Perigo for a start.

Perigo was Small Heath born and bred – or even bread because, instead of working for his family's bakery, Bert drove vans for Bordesley Engineering of New Bond Street, which had been producing motorcycles under the Connaught banner since 1912. Perigo persuaded them to enter him in the London to Edinburgh 24-hour trial, which he won, securing his first of many ACU gold medals. When Bordesley Engineering closed in 1926 Perigo moved to BSA and joined the competitions department, winning the inaugural British Experts Trial in 1929 and representing Britain in ISDTs, and winning a gold medal at the 1931 event in Merano, Italy.

In 1937 Perigo rode a B25 Empire Star to victory in both the Colmore Cup and Victory Cup trials. His success was so important to BSA in developing the BSA Blue Star range that he was paid a halfpenny royalty for every Blue Star sold. He was also instrumental in Wal Handley's 1937 lapping of Brooklands at over 100mph (160km/h) on an Empire Star. More prosaically Perigo had also instigated a testing programme of using inexperienced riders to test new models, reasoning that they were more likely to treat the bikes as they might be treated by the buying public.

The prospect of standard road bikes competing in a specialist mixed road condition trial appealed to the ACU, which hadn't awarded the Maudes Trophy since 1939. So on 30 August 1952, the ACU picked at random three Star Twins from BSA's assembly line for the Maudes Trophy attempt. The riders undertaking the challenge were Norman Vanhouse, Fred Rist and Brian Martin, who first had to ride from Birmingham to Bad Aussee in Austria for the ISDT. For those unfamiliar with an ISDT, some 200 miles (320km) a day are covered over the roughest and most varied road conditions, including steep climbs. And of course, the further you fall behind the leaders, the muddier and more torn up the track surfaces become. It rained continuously, as it often does in Austria. On one climb, a track in the middle of a forest, the tyre tracks of previous competitors had made the route impassable and necessitated a detour.

The editorial in *Motor Cycling*'s 25 September issue was headlined 'Bad News From Bad Aussee' and reported dolefully that...

> *...these words are being written while we still await the final confirmed results of the International Six Days Trial. It seems evident that things have by no means gone as planned by Great Britain. Until our representatives return home it will not be possible to establish a clear picture of what went wrong and, in any case, this is not the moment to conduct a post mortem. Rather it is one to congratulate the winners on their success, to compliment the organisers on what seems to have been a difficult yet fair trial, and to commiserate with those who found that their luck was Out.*

The Czechoslovakian team were the winners, their lightweight 250cc Jawa two-stroke singles far more suitable for the conditions than big British four-stroke singles, never mind the BSA (and Royal Enfield, Matchless, AJS and Triumph) twins. But confidence, ability and a good machine worked wonders, and the three Star Twins were awarded the gold medals that participants who finished within 10 per cent of their class winner's total time got to take home. They were also the only British team to finish with clean sheets – that is, without penalties.

Under normal circumstances the three riders and A7s would have chosen a direct route home, but instead they travelled to Oslo, where they undertook some flying quarter miles to record average speeds over 80mph (130km/h). Nigh on 5,000 miles (8,000km) had been covered in twenty-two days, including those six days of concentrated ISDT punishment, both physical and mechanical, before the eventual return to Small Heath.

On their return to the factory the engines were stripped and examined, again under ACU supervision, with almost minimal wear and tear recorded. The ACU men had no doubts in awarding the Maudes Trophy to BSA for the third and final time, thirteen years after their last win. And there the trophy stayed, despite many efforts, for some time. It would be 1962 before the trophy was awarded again, when three standard production Honda 50cc Supercubs (a C100, a C102 and a C110) with a team of twenty riders covered more than 15,800 miles (25,400km) at Goodwood in a week long, day and night continuous test. The last time the Maudes Trophy was awarded was in 1994, seemingly because the industry, rather than the ACU, had lost interest in that type of endurance challenge, and probably because motorcycles are now so reliable.

Later Golden Flash with swinging arm rear suspension.

Jerry Garrett with his 1963 BSA Rocket Gold Star. CRAIG HOWELL

TUNING THE TWINS

On a 1951 visit to the US, chief designer Bert Hopwood discovered – to no one's surprise – that more powerful motorcycles would sell well. The competitions department had tuned the A7 for the Daytona 200, and Fred Rist had an A10 desert racer reputedly capable of 140mph (225km/h). Gene Thiessen set an AMA class B record at the Bonneville saltflats of 151mph (243km/h) in October 1951 and, in 1952, American BSA dealer Hap Alzina built a Star Twin for an attempt on the American Class C speed record for standard motorcycles. Thiessen set a two-way record of 123.69mph (199.06 km/h).

Armed with this experience, and with judicious picking from BSA's options list, Hopwood came up with the A10 Super Flash, aimed at giving American riders the extra power they craved and creating a homologation special. The specification included a 357 race camshaft and Amal TT carburettor to boost power to 40bhp. The carburettor required a curved seat post and the frame also had lugs for rearset footrests. A Gold Star tank – with 'Super Flash' decal – and chrome mudguards completed the look.

The first Super Flash was shipped to the US in February 1953, with *American Motorcycling* magazine making it 'Motor of the Month'. Production ended in 1954 with a handful of swinging arm models, some 700 Super Flashes having been made. The motor later powered the Ariel Cyclone.

The Super Flash was replaced at the top of BSA's range in 1954 with the Road Rocket, the first A10 with an alloy cylinder head. This also dropped the integral inlet manifold, allowing twin carburettors to be fitted, although standard fitment was a single Amal TT. The cylinder and big ends were beefed up, and high compression pistons and a 356 sports camshaft were fitted. Claimed power remained at 40bhp, but of course there was now the possibility of fitting twin carburettors.

The Super Rocket replaced the Road Rocket in 1958, retaining the Amal TT carburettor and 356 camshafts. Compression was raised to 8.5:1, and a new alloy cylinder head was fitted with larger ports and valves. The crankshaft was strengthened to cope with a claimed power increase to 43bhp. Full width brakes were also new but remained 8in and 7in, front and rear respectively. For 1960 a 357 race camshaft was fitted and the clutch was improved. A larger

Brochure for the BSA Super Flash 650.

ABOVE: **Inside the Super Flash brochure – the (American) public gets what the (American) public wants.**

The 1963 A10 Super Rocket. MF HUTCHINS

A Norbsa – a Norton featherbed frame with pre-unit BSA twin.

A 1957 BSA Spitfire with owner John Batchler and show host.

CRAIG HOWELL

$1^{5}/_{32}$in (29mm) Monobloc carburettor appeared in 1962, boosting the claimed output to 46bhp.

The Rocket Gold Star (also known as the Gold Star Twin) was introduced in 1962, a Super Rocket engine in a Gold Star frame. Gold Star tuner and dealer, Eddie Dow, had built such a hybrid for a customer and BSA decided to put the model into limited production. Options such as an Amal GP2 carburettor and Siamesed exhaust pipes could increase power to 50bhp, but alongside a close-ratio RRT2 gearbox, this added 30 per cent to the price. Production ended in 1963.

The Spitfire Scrambler was introduced in 1957 at the request of BSA's West Coast distributor, Hap Alzina, squarely aimed at beating the dominant Triumph twins in desert racing. Very much a competition model, no lights or silencers were fitted, and there was a Lucas competition magneto. The engine was based on the Road Rocket's, the

The 1960 500 Shooting Star. SG2012

head modified to allow a $1^1/_{16}$in (27mm) Amal Monobloc: compression was 9:1, and a 357 race camshaft was fitted. Initially the frame, forks and wheels were from the Gold Star Catalina, but during 1957 it reverted to an A10 frame.

For 1958 the engine was fitted with the Super Rocket's 'big valve' head, and the following year there was a shorter seat and high level exhausts. Production ended in 1963 after it was merged with the Road Gold Star Scrambler and renamed the Gold Star Spitfire Scrambler.

NOT FORGETTING THE 500

The A7 Shooting Star was introduced in 1954 with a new swinging arm frame and a hotter camshaft, and compression was raised to 7:1, giving 30bhp. The alloy cylinder head, like the sportier A10s, allowed twin carburettors, and the front brake grew to 8in. In 1954 Bobby Hill won the Daytona 200 riding a rigid-framed Shooting Star, by then a special order from the factory. Of the 107 starters only forty-four finished, with Shooting Stars claiming first, second, fourth and fifth places. A BSA Gold Star finished third.

We will return to the BSA twins, which would become an important part of the company's later post-war history. Yes, they were important earlier, but in the immediate post-war period, BSA was still very much famous for its four-stroke singles.

THE A7 AND A10

Year: 1946 (substantially revised 1951-on version in brackets/A10)
Power: 35bhp at 4,500rpm
Weight: 179kg (395lb)
Displacement: 495cc (497cc/646cc)
Bore/stroke: 62 x 82mm (66 x 72.6mm/70 x 84mm)
Compression ratio: 6:1 (6.7:1)
Engine type: Four-stroke overhead-valve vertical twin
Carburation: Single Amal
Ignition system: Lucas magneto
Claimed power: 26bhp (28/35bhp)
Transmission: Multiplate wet clutch, four-speed semi-unit gearbox. Primary and final drive by chain
Brakes: 7in single leading shoe front (7/8in) and rear
Wheels: 19in; 3.25in front, 3.50in rear
Chassis: Telescopic front forks, rigid or plunger rear, half duplex frame
Weight: 167kg/369lb
Top speed: 80–85mph/ 130–136km/h (85/95mph)

CHAPTER SIX

RESTARTING THE SINGLES

Although BSA ostensibly put all their energies into supplying the War Office during World War II, by 1944, in a small building in Redditch away from the ministry men at Small Heath, BSA were developing the machines they would introduce when peace was declared. The first of these, the B31, was based on the B29 Silver Sports introduced in 1940. Only a few had been sold before BSA turned to the war effort, and the B29 evolved into the B30, a prototype 350 for the military. And then the War Office decided they already had a wide enough variety of motorcycles, leaving the B30 stillborn. Post war the project would resurface as the civilian B31.

There were two significant differences between the B29/B30 and the 1945 B31. The most obvious was BSA's own telescopic front forks, which replaced the girders of pre-war models. And under the guidance of Edward Turner, coil valve

The 1948 B31. Contrast this to the later version in the next photo. SG2012

A late B33, looking very different to the original version based on the B31.

springs replaced hairpins for a more compact cylinder head.

The B31 also had a stronger crankcase than BSA's pre-war Empire Star, although the early B31s probably owed much to that motorcycle, being more lightweight than subsequent versions, and sitting lower to the ground. The speedo was in the tank, and the first B31s carried over war-time features such as different levers and front forks without a drain plug. The semi-cradle frame was soon made stronger, even though it was still smaller than the M20's. There were no sidecar lugs, as the M20 and M21 remained BSA's suggested sidecar luggers.

The civilian M20 was available immediately after the war with minor changes, most noticeably the absence of khaki paint. The new B31, along with the revised pre-war 250 C10 and C11, only became available in September and October 1945. However, nearly all were for export only and, with a huge national debt to repay, very few new vehicles were for sale in Britain.

The B31's 71 x 88mm bore and stroke displaced 348cc, initially in a rigid frame with BSA's first telescopic forks and, with about 17bhp, could reach some 70mph (112km/h). It sold well and was soon joined by a 499cc big bore (85mm) version, the B33. There were also the B32 and B34 competition models and then sidecar equivalents prefixed with an extra B. Plunger rear suspension was offered later, with a swingarm rear suspension frame available from 1954. The model continued in production until 1959, by which time the traditional Lucas magdyno had been replaced by alternator and coil ignition.

The B range expanded through its life to include the famous Gold Stars, the bottom half of all the ohv pre-unit singles having much in common with the M-series side-valve versions. The M33, designed for sidecar work, combined the stronger M-series frame with the more powerful B33 500 motor.

THE GOLD STAR

The first Gold Star was the pre-war M24 model, with an aluminium alloy 496cc engine, a magnesium alloy gearbox, and a rigid frame made of light tubes without sidecar attachment lugs, unusual for BSA. The name was adopted to remember Wal Handley's 1937 race at Brooklands, lapping at over 100mph (160km/h) on an Empire Star, being awarded one of the traditional gold star pins for the achievement.

BSA launched the 348cc ZB32 Gold Star in 1948 (for the 1949 season) at a price of £211, soon joined by the shorter stroke, marginally enlarged 499cc '500' ZB34 Gold Star, with an upgraded main bearing and crankshaft, but with the same

The 1938 M24 Gold Star, origin of the species. BONHAMS

hand-built attention to detail. Superseding the B32 and B34 Competition models, these Gold Stars had plunger frames but could still be ordered with a rigid frame as the ZB31 and ZB33 respectively. In order to satisfy the eligibility requirements for the Clubmans TT, over 100 machines had to be produced, twenty-one of which were entered into the 1949 Junior, a race to be dominated by ZB32 Gold Stars for the next eight years, until the final Clubmans TT races in 1956.

The ACU had introduced the Clubmans category when the TT resumed in 1947, intended for near-standard roadsters: entrants had to retain lights and kick starters, and megaphones were prohibited. There were three classes – Lightweight, Junior and Senior – within a single race, although the Lightweight competitors completed only three laps of the mountain course rather than four of the Junior and Senior.

The all-alloy (engine and gearbox castings) Gold Stars were offered with a long list of options: owners could specify camshafts, compression ratio, carburettor, cylinder head, exhaust, gearbox ratios, lighting, tyres and electrical systems. The components were carefully selected from stock, and the bikes skilfully assembled by hand with the engine bench tested. They were 9kg (20lb) lighter than the equivalent B series with its cast-iron barrel and head, and could be specified in tourer, trials, ISDT, scrambling, road racing or Clubmans trim.

Despite the presence of overhead cam Nortons and Velocettes, the 1949 Clubmans Junior TT was won by Harold Clark on a Gold Star, and ZB32s would win every Clubmans Junior TT from then on, often filling the podium. Indeed, by the final event in 1956, the first twenty-two motorcycles home were Gold Stars.

For 1950 a bigger front brake was fitted, and for 1952 the 500 Goldie gained a new cylinder head, designed by Bert Hopwood. The 350 adopted the new head the following year, and BSA made many detail changes to keep the bikes competitive.

BUILDING AND RACING THE GOLD STAR: STAN DIBBEN'S STORY

On a sunny April afternoon I met Stan Dibben and his son Mark at Avebury, the magnificent stone circle with a fine National Trust café set about halfway between our respective homes in the Wiltshire countryside. Stan

The 1954 499cc Gold Star Trials. BONHAMS

might have worked at BSA for only two years, but he was at the heart of the factory's Gold Star shop, and also worked alongside the experimental and competition departments. He subsequently spent a lifetime in the British motorcycle industry, recording his experiences of the business models in a fascinatingly anecdotal book co-authored with his son Mark, who drove Stan over. Their book, *Enterprise on the Edge of Industry*, is a fine examination of Stan's career viewed through the prism of Mark's academic studies and business consultancy. But perhaps most impressively, having been instructed by Norton's Joe Craig to act as 'ballast' for Eric Oliver at a MIRA test session, Stan found himself seconded to his sidecar for the 1953 season. They won the world championship, Oliver's fourth and final title in the class. No wonder Stan's autobiography is titled *Hold On!*

Stan joined BSA in 1949. His trial riding had 'caught the eye of Ralph Venables as a potential guinea pig and development rider'. Stan had been finishing an electrical apprenticeship at the SEB (Southern Electricity Board), interrupted by service with the Royal Navy in Canada during the war, but he wanted to make motorcycling his career. 'Ralph suggested writing to Bert Perigo, and I got a reply by return with a job offer and lodgings! I was going straight into building Gold Stars – I think someone must have put in a good word!' Stan smiles.

Perigo was a British engineer who had been a successful motorcycle trials rider before becoming competition manager for BSA. Clearly Venables had seen Stan's potential and wanted to make sure BSA harnessed it, the Birmingham factory considering off-road sport its most important marketing effort. This was unusual for a British factory, most of which saw road racing – and the TT in particular – as the way to a buyer's heart. But in BSA's TT debut in 1921 all six factory machines had failed to finish and, from then on, the company looked to off-road sport, in all its variety, to prove the worth of their single-cylinder machines.

Prime of these was the legendary Gold Star in 350 and 500cc capacities, hand built in a small workshop more reminiscent of racing teams and smaller companies such as Velocette. Each member of the team of eight would usually assemble one bike a day, collecting what was needed from the stores shortly after clocking on. It was to this élite team that Stan was recruited, led by former New Imperial TT rider Sammy Jones. To these nine men one can add the name of tester Lol Statham.

> *I rode up on my first day on my G3LC Matchless, my trial bike. It had no lights, but there wasn't much traffic. Took about two hours from my home in Hampshire – it was October, very cold. I went straight to my digs at Omebersley Road. They were the comedy variety – you'd swop the bed with a bloke going off to a night shift. I wasn't happy with that and only lasted a week. One of the other Gold Star builders – Stuart McLeod, a very well educated Geordie – got me a place at 202 Charles Road. You could walk to the factory easily. David Tye [works off-road rider] and Geoff Duke would stay there.*
>
> *We'd start each day by going and seeing Sammy to get the spec of the bike we were building and the engine number. Then I'd go to the store where they'd have picked out, in most cases, some special parts. They could be expensive. I built Fred Rist's [UK team captain] Six Day Gold Star.*

Although BSA had a canteen, the Gold Star team chose to keep to themselves for the most part.

> *The Gold Star shop was totally separate and very family orientated. We would sit down together with sandwiches – usually cheese. We'd go to the cinema together every two weeks, just to watch whatever was on. Of course that was the way it was. We'd ride out from the factory on the tramlines and whoever slid off first paid for the tickets. Every other night we'd go to play snooker at the very good [Birmingham] motorcycle club, just a hundred yards from BSA's front door. Other evenings Stuart and I would visit Olga Kevelos' [the only woman to win two gold medals in International Six Day Trials] Cherry Orchard Café in the middle of Birmingham. She was friendly with [Featherbed frame] designer Rex McCandless, which is how I met him.*
>
> *I'll give you an idea of how much of a family we were. When I went back to SEB after the war nobody asked what it had been like for me or why I was in Canada. [But in the Gold Star shop] we were very apart from the main factory, and nobody in management cared what anyone building the bikes thought. The sales manager was walking around and I told him the [higher] Western handlebars were all the go in the US and Canada [at the time when most*

Stan Dibben in the BSA Gold Star shop.
COLLECTION OF STAN DIBBEN

Gold Stars were bought for off road competition]. But he couldn't see using anything else [other than the handlebars we were already using] probably because they'd been designed and built in house. I showed him some, but he just said `we wouldn't sanction handlebars like that'. Of course he disproved of the coloured beaded seats the Americans were fitting. It makes me realize the freedom that we had [in the Gold Star shop]. It was fabulous, especially when I went to Norton.

Another thing that set us apart was we were horrified at the stiff-legged walk a lot of people had as they walked past security at the end of every day. Clearly they had fork legs down their trousers but no one got stopped. The thieving was horrendous. And the main factory was like the Mafia, every family looking after their own, even at the expense of the company. If a job came up in a particular part of the factory you knew it would go to whoever the people who already worked their thought should have it. If you didn't know them there it was pointless applying for the job.

The directors weren't interested in motorcycles. They thought that you had to know how to be a director of a company, not about the things the factory made. Gilbert Smith [at Norton] was more interested in Arkell's [brewery of which he was also a directory].

The experimental department was the only other place like [the Gold Star shop], a family. Like us no-one there would dream of nicking stuff. I got to know Bill Nicholson there [arguably the factory's first star rider and a brilliant frame designer] who'd lend bikes just wanting miles put on them. I rode them home to Ropley [in east Hampshire] on Friday evenings and then back on Sunday afternoon, about 130 miles each way. I got a bit quicker as I got used to it. Then [department head] Len Crisp would ask me to take development bikes. They might have had different pistons in them, I never knew. Looking back it's strange I was never asked what I thought of bikes. They just wanted miles putting on them, more interested in wear and reliability rather than wanting to make the bikes better to ride. A 650 Golden Flash, a B31, B34, even 400 miles on a Bantam. If they'd had a rolling road I wouldn't have had them for the weekend.

I was riding in weekend trials too. I won the newcomer's award in the Calcutt Trial, my first event after arriving in the Midlands riding my Matchless. It caused quite a stir at the factory and the motorcycle club. By now Stuart McLeod was almost a big brother influence and he encouraged me to have a go at road racing.

Sammy Jones was wonderful to me. He let me build myself a 350 Gold Star in 1951. On hire purchase of course. It was a bit special: lightened frame lugs, all black, no chrome. The only all black Gold Star ever to leave the factory. That was my favourite Gold Star: I used it as a hack to learn the TT Isle of Man course when I went there to race for Norton. I did about forty laps on it.

My first race [with the 350 Gold Star] was at Chelmsford. I fell off chasing Keith Campbell. I'd get sixths and sevenths in fields of thirty to thirty-five. I got a second at Thruxton that Rex McCandless saw, and after that he poached me for Norton's Experimental Department. I joined in October 1952 on £7 a week. I was on £5 a week at BSA for a 52½ hour week. Of course we all stayed in touch. I smuggled Stuart McLeod into Norton one night to help me build my Manx 350.

FINALLY – A SWINGING-ARM FRAME

Pat Slinn, who would go on to spanner for Tony Rutter and Mike Hailwood at the TT, remembers seeing George Formby's *No Limit* at the cinema on his first visit to the Isle of Man in 1948. Just five years old, he was there, along with his parents and twin brother Mike, as moral support for his father, Reg, a BSA engineer working for the development and experimental department. But Reg wasn't just a theorist, he was racing a ZB Gold Star with a Rex McCandless (of Norton Featherbed fame) experimental swinging arm in the Clubmans Junior TT. Although Pat laughs now, he remembers being quite upset after watching *No Limit*:

We saw all the crashes, and thought 'that's what's going to happen to Dad!' We must have watched the start from the grandstand, because I can remember all the noise and the bikes all together. There were lots of people, even in those days, and I thought it was wonderful. My memories are pretty mixed up – I was only five – but I remember having to wait on Douglas Prom most of the last day because we'd had to check out of the Mona Hotel in the morning and wait for a late ferry. In those days there were boating pools along the front – they're flowerbeds now – and Mike managed to fall into one. Mum stripped him off and laid his clothes out on the wall to dry!

Although Reg Slinn failed to finish his race, the swinging-arm frame continued to be developed. The new swing-arm frame in 1953 ushered in more success, including the 1954 Clubmans Senior TT, which was won by Eddie Dow.

The swinging-arm frame is generally credited to brothers Rex and Cromie McCandless, who offered Norton a new frame to support their successful 500cc race single no later than 1949. Rex McCandless was a self-taught Belfast motorcycle engineer and raced competitively with his brother on a Triumph Tiger 100. This machine was notable for an innovative new frame with a swinging arm fitted with vertical hydraulic shock absorbers from a Citroen car. BSA had bought several of McCandless's converted motorcycles, but it was Norton's Joe Craig who saw the real opportunity and contracted Rex to work exclusively for them from 1949.

Norton commissioned the McCandless brothers to design a complete frame, incorporating a swinging arm. In two months a prototype motorcycle with the new frame was on the test track, and it was tested on the Isle of Man in the winter of 1949. It performed well, and Norton applied for a patent on the design on 13 October 1949 – but the completed specification wasn't published until 9 January 1952. By then BSA was almost ready to announce their own version.

That this rear suspension was viewed with suspicion until Moto Guzzi proved its worth seems incomprehensible now, as does the crudeness of plunger rear suspension. But these were easy and cheap options for a rigid frame, whereas a swinging-arm frame required more substantial alterations and Norton invoked an all-new design that was expensive to produce and required far greater lengths of tubing. On the other hand BSA's new duplex cradle swinging-arm frame was essentially a stock all-welded B33 frame, albeit one with revised lugs and brackets, with the precious GS (Gold Star) prefix to the frame number.

Front suspension was by BSA's competent if unremarkable single damped telescopic fork, while at the rear a brace of Girling dampers controlled the swinging arm. This was

Reg Slinn at the 1948 TT with BSA's experimental swinging arm frame. COLLECTION OF PAT SLINN

BELOW: **The 1956 DBD34 Gold Star Daytona, still available with a rigid frame.** YESTERDAYS ANTIQUE MOTORCYCLES

The look everyone associates with the Gold Star name, a DBD34 with RRT2 gearbox.

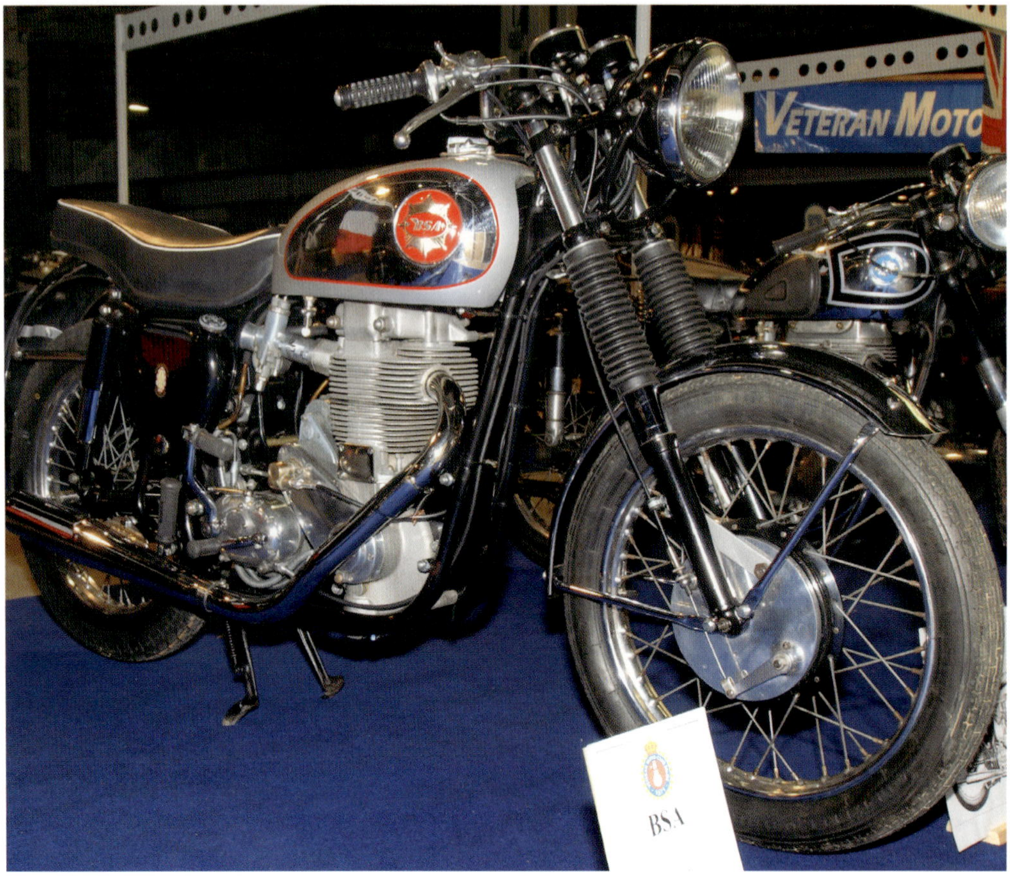

The 1957 350 Gold Star.

ALF VAN BEEM

designated the BB, and customers could specify this state of tune for a couple of years. The CB models arrived in 1954 with a new engine featuring additional, square finning, a shorter conrod, stronger crank, oval flywheels for the 500, modified valve gear, Amal GP carb and a swept-back exhaust.

But the United States was still the most important market, so in 1954, BSA brought a team to the Daytona 200-mile race with a mix of Gold Stars and Shooting Star twins assembled by Roland Pike. They took the first five places, plus eighth and sixteenth, and Gold Stars were also dominating off-road racing, motocross, scrambling and desert racing well past 1963 when production ended.

Then for 1955 came the DB models, with improved crankshaft oil feed, finned front drum brake and a special silencer that was paired to the Clubman models' cams and timing. For a short while it was possible to specify either BB, CB or DB engines, until the earlier types were discontinued at the end of 1955 when the final – and many say the ultimate – Gold Star arrived, the DBD34. This introduced a modified cylinder head, based upon its CB predecessor, but revised for the DBD to accommodate one of the largest carburettors available, the 1½in (38mm) Amal GP item. It featured shallower valve angles and a slightly larger inlet valve with

DB GOLD STAR 34 (32 IN BRACKETS WHERE DIFFERENT)

Year: 1961
Displacement: 499cc (348cc)
Bore/stroke: 85 x 88mm (71 x 85mm)
Compression ratio: 8:1 (8.75:1)
Engine type: Four-stroke overhead-valve vertical single
Carburation: Single Amal GP – typically 1½in (38mm)
Ignition system: Lucas magneto
Claimed power: 38bhp at 7,000rpm
Transmission: Multiplate wet clutch, four-speed non-unit gearbox. Primary and final drive by chain
Brakes: 8in single leading shoe drum front, 7in single leading shoe drum rear
Wheels: 21in (19in)
Chassis: Telescopic front forks, Girling twin shock absorber rear swinging arm, half duplex frame
Weight: 383lb (380lb) /174kg (172kg)
Top speed: Dependent on specification, but over 100mph (160km/h)

Not everybody leaves their BSA single standard.

The Catalina decal on the tank was applied at the factory. BONHAMS

1961 BSA 500cc Gold Star Catalina Scrambler. BONHAMS

1954 B33 in period.
STEVE SHRIVER

the inlet tract reduced to provide a 'turbulence lip', claimed to improve performance. BSA's racing 190mm (7½in) full-width front brake was also an option. Available in both Clubmans and Scrambles trim for £277, but without roadster or touring options, the Gold Star was now very much a competition-only model.

Along with the DBD came the famous RRT2 gearbox: RR for ultra-close ratio, T for Torrington needle-roller bearings, and a two because needle-roller sets were fitted in both the sleeve gear and at either end of the layshaft. The clutch (and later the drive chains) was also beefed up to handle the power increase. There remained many options and, theoretically, a standard gearbox (stamped STD rather than RRT2) could be ordered, although with only four speeds it would make the highly tuned engine unusable.

Even as it reached the end of its life, the Gold Star could pull something special out of the bag. A Californian race created yet another variant, one of its most famous, for the increasingly important US market. In 1956 Chuck Minert fitted a 5gal (22.7ltr) fuel tank, an air-scooped front brake and 19in front wheel on to his DB34 scrambler, and promptly won the prestigious Catalina Grand Prix ahead of almost 1,000 other riders on Catalina Island, off the California coast. BSA west coast distributor Hap Alzina immediately lobbied the factory for a production replica of Minert's winning bike. The result was the Gold Star Catalina Scrambler.

Despite this, and although the Gold Star remained competitive – notably in the hands of future world champion Jeff Smith – BSA's top brass seemed to lose interest in the Goldie after the Isle of Man Clubman TT was ended in 1956. When a frustrated Alzina warned that he would not order any more BSAs until they supplied him with more Gold Stars, it is said that someone at the top end of BSA averred: 'If he won't buy what we want to make, we'll stop making what he wants to buy' – and they did.

Officially the reason for the Gold Star's demise was that Lucas Electrics had stopped making magnetos and BSA was running out of their stockpile. In truth, despite a brilliant career and incredible success both in competition and in the showroom, the Gold Star had run its race. When Lucas, cynically nicknamed Prince of Darkness for their unreliability, showed BSA the door it was a perfect excuse to bring an era to an end. The last Gold Star rolled off the line in 1963, a year before Jeff Smith's first world championship.

It was replaced in 1964 with a new line of unit-construction singles led by the B50, a development of the C15, the first BSA unit singles. While more modern in every way, these failed to generate the kind of affection and respect that the Gold Star had deservedly attracted.

CHAPTER SEVEN

THE POLITICS OF GROWTH – AND SEEDS OF FAILURE

BSA's plans for post-war domination carried on apace with purchases of Sunbeam, Ariel and, eventually, Triumph. First blood came in 1943 when the group bought the Sunbeam name from AMC (Associated Motorcycles, famous for owning AJS and Matchless and, later, Norton) but abandoned Sunbeam's association with TT-winning singles. Instead the all-new S models were designed for BSA by Erling Poppe, inspired by BMW flat twins obtained as war reparations. Manufactured at Redditch from 1946 to 1956, there were three models: the S7, S8 and S7 Deluxe. All were expensive but with only modest performance, which, along with shaft drive and great comfort, presumably were a pre-emptive

BSA had no interest in reviving Sunbeam's reputation for sporting singles such as this.

The 1949 Sunbeam S7 Deluxe. SID MOSDELL

The 1950 Sunbeam S8. TONY HISGETT

challenge to BMW's return to the civilian market post war. This can also be inferred by BSA's instructions to Poppe that the machine mustn't look 'too German'. It is also worth adding here that BSA turned down the opportunity to build the VW Beetle in the UK, believing that their focus on Daimler would be more lucrative.

The Sunbeam S7's unusual engine layout took a longitudinally mounted vertical overhead camshaft (ohc) 487cc parallel twin with shaft drive to the rear wheel. Unlike BMW, however, who wisely specified a bevel gear crown and pinion drive to the rear wheel, Sunbeam used worm gearing with a bronze spiral gear, and the S7 quickly gained a reputation for the soft bronze allowing rapid wear of drive components. Such reliability issues and a high price contributed to disappointing sales.

The original S7 was replaced in 1949 with the sportier S8, with larger wheels rather than the fat, squat tyres of the S7, and updated with BSA front forks. The S7 was upgraded to the S7 Deluxe: although the early S7 was not a good seller or mechanically especially sound, it is the most sought after and commands a premium over the S7 Deluxe and the S8 with collectors today. S7 and S8 production ended in 1956, although BSA would relaunch Sunbeam as a scooter brand in 1959.

COMETH THE HOUR, COMETH THE MAN: JACK SANGSTER

BSA's part in Ariel's history, and subsequently Triumph's, is tied up with one man who would go on to become BSA's chairman. Born John Young Sangster in 1896, but known to all as Jack, he would become an important enough figurehead in the British motorcycle industry to be offered a peerage – which, remarkably, he declined. Despite this, and the fact that he was one of the few men at the top of BSA who had any sort of engineering background – and despite his philanthropy, and taking in two London evacuees in 1944 – Sangster was not universally admired.

Born in Kings Norton, Birmingham, the son of Charles Thomas Brock Sangster – engineer, and bicycle and motorcycle pioneer – Jack was educated at Hurstpierpoint College, Sussex. He moved on to an engineering apprenticeship interrupted by World War I. During the war Sangster served with the City of Birmingham battalion of the 14th Royal Warwickshire Regiment. His elder brother Fredrick Charles Sangster was killed in action.

Returning from war in 1918, Jack joined Components Ltd, where his father was managing director. Here Jack designed and built a small, low cost car, later sold to Rover, with Sangster following it to manage production of what would became the Rover Model Eight. Conspiracy theorists can start here on the genesis of the 1950s feud between Sangster and BSA's then chairman Bernard Docker. Docker tied his and BSA's success to Daimler cars, something most observers have considered one of the early failings in BSA's management, which started its fall from grace. Readers may recall that it was Sir Bernard's father, Dudley, who had brought Daimler into the BSA fold, choosing it over Rover. The rise of Rover as Daimler struggled must have grated with the Dockers. That Sangster, as an engineer – hardly the occupation of a gentleman – had a part in Rover's success must have informed the Dockers' opinion of the man.

In 1923 Sangster returned to his father's company, and by 1930 he was joint managing director. But in 1932 Components Ltd went bust, as many did during those days of the Great Depression. Sangster bought most of the company's assets from the receivers, rebuilding the company using the wealth of design and engineering talent employed by the company, which included Edward Turner, Val Page and Bert Hopwood. He called the new company Ariel Motors (JS) Ltd.

Despite the perilous state of the world economy, Sangster then bought the bankrupt Triumph motorcycles in 1935, setting Edward Turner and Bert Hopwood the task of improving Triumph's product range. The Triumph Speed Twin, designed by Turner, with its parallel twin engine, was the blueprint of a line of successful Triumph motorcycles – indeed the entire British motorcycle industry's model lineup – that would follow.

Again, readers may recall that there were certain grudges here. Val Page would join BSA in 1936, having left Ariel in 1932 to become chief designer at rivals Triumph where, with Edward Turner, he developed Triumph's first parallel twin, the model 6/1. But once installed at Triumph, Page discovered he couldn't get on with Turner, who in turn bore a grudge against BSA: the Triumph twin was effectively half of Turner's 1928 Square Four design that BSA had rejected and Ariel eventually picked up.

For his new Ariel motorcycles Sangster set up shop at Selly Oak in Birmingham, with one of its first models – the Square Four – appearing first for 1931 as an ohc 500. The company again collapsed, revived to first build a revised

601cc Square Four, with a more substantial revision in 1937 reinventing the 'Squariel' (as it became known) as a 995cc ohv model designated the 4G. The easier-to-cool overhead-valve layout replaced the overhead camshaft of the earlier models in an attempt to prevent the perpetual problem of the rear cylinder head overheating. These overheating problems resulted in distorted heads, even with a switch from cast-iron to alloy castings, blighting the motor throughout its life.

Inevitably the Square Four was always a large, expensive motorcycle, and its slow death was finally delivered in 1959. Nonetheless it was revived in the 1970s as the Healey 1000/4, a creation of Squariel fans George and Tim Healey. The two bought up as many Ariel Square Four parts as they could, and set about creating the ultimate Ariel Square Four motorcycle, based on a good deal of experience modifying them for racing and sprint racing. Sadly the Healeys' optimism was misplaced, although they did find minor fame as producers of the early Laverda Jota's exhaust system.

ARIEL'S HUNTERS

The Square Four was followed by the altogether more successful Red Hunter. Penned by chief designer Val Page, it was announced in 1932 but based on an ohv single he had developed some six years earlier. 500, 350 and 250 versions were developed and became especially popular with grass track and trials riders. The Red Hunter became the hit single that funded Ariel's purchase of Triumph and would form the basis for Sammy Miller's 1955 trials motorcycle, which proved astoundingly successful in competition.

During World War II the Ariel factory was turned over to military production, including the Ariel W/NG 350 for the army, based on the Red Hunter but with increased ground clearance. As the war drew to a close, Sangster sold Ariel to BSA for a sizeable profit, followed, in 1951, by Triumph for £2.5 million, plus a place on the BSA board. Not a bad return on the £50,000 Sangster had paid for Triumph in 1935.

Ariel's final four-stroke fling was the 500cc KH Fieldmas-

Red Hunter 500, the Ariel that made the profits. STEFFEN HEINZ CARONNA

The Fieldmaster, the Ariel with a BSA motor. BONHAMS

ter twin, again designed by Page, produced between 1948 and 1957. At launch Ariel's new twin seemed to have a bright future, with a top speed of around 90mph (145km/h), the Fieldmaster as fast as a BSA A7 or Triumph Speed Twin, and a real eye-catcher with its red-and-chrome petrol tank. A sister model – the slightly less powerful KG De Luxe – was available in black. Although Page's design was similar in layout to Turner's Speed Twin, using the same 63 x 80mm bore and stroke, it differed greatly in detail, particularly in the bottom end. This prevented stretching it to the 650cc the market soon demanded and, understandably, BSA simply produced a version of its A10 twin as the 1954 Ariel Huntmaster. Reliable and capable of 100mph (160km/h), the Huntmaster proved popular with sidecar enthusiasts.

To add to this sudden grasp of rationalization, BSA started fitting Ariel's superior brakes to their own branded models. That this is remarkable perhaps shows Sangster's greatest weakness: his affection for, and deference to Turner. In 1941 Sangster had fired Turner from Ariel for insubordination, but BSA quickly hired him and Sangster felt he'd made a grave error by handing Turner over to the competition. So he rehired Turner in 1943 as general manager – on Edward's own terms – and forever after Turner could – and would – do as he pleased.

So while Ariel was increasingly and rationally brought into Small Heath's orbit, with thought given to how Ariel and BSA fitted into the market place to complement rather than compete with one another, Triumph and Turner were almost allowed to go rogue. Fans might point to Turner and Triumph's remarkable talent for staying one step ahead of the market and competition, but the factionalization at Meriden, and the eventual infighting between Triumph and BSA 750 triples' teams, especially, was part of this and undoubtedly contributed to BSA's demise.

In the meantime, for 1959, Ariel dropped its four-stroke engines and gambled the future on the Leader, a fully enclosed 250 two-stroke with fully faired bodywork. The Leader aimed to combine the performance of a motorcycle with the convenience of a scooter, and at first it sold well – in 1959 it won the *Motor*

The 1963 Ariel Leader, the bike BSA thought would revive Ariel. MICK FROM NORTHAMPTONSHIRE

Cycle News Motorcycle of the Year award. But once the initial novelty died down, the Leader appealed to neither motorcycle nor scooter fans. Ariel's response was the Arrow, a less faired-in – 'naked' – version of the Leader, but which kept the Leader's enclosed chain case and deep mudguards. Both models proved unsuccessful, especially in the face of Japanese imports.

BSA closed the Ariel factory at Selly Oak in 1962 and moved production to Small Heath. Production of the 50cc Ariel Pixie began in 1963, but by then Ariel motorcycles existed in name only. For now, all that can be said is that Ariel produced its last motorcycle in 1965, the Arrow 200 with capacity reduced to 199.6cc (from 1964) to qualify for lower UK rider insurance and taxes. Ariel ceased production in 1967, although the name would be revived with an infamous trike in the 1970s – but that's still some way off in our story.

TRIUMPH IN THE BOARDROOM

As mentioned in the introduction, part of this tale of 'The BSA' will be to try and understand how the mighty fell. It is really in this period that the seeds of destruction were sown, and salvation became almost impossible within a decade. It is telling that talking to accountants would have uncovered little but good news and, across British industry, all looked well until almost the end. Perhaps even the finest and most experienced directors and managers would have been blind-sided by unpredictable government policies that constantly sought to raise new taxes – often deliberately unpredictable and so unavoidable – on fuel, purchases and company profits.

Governments also, just like British industry, were gripped by a Britain-is-unbeatable hubris, unable to believe that its own citizens would choose to buy imported goods over home-grown produce. And the accounts supported this: in 1966 BSA was the UK's top US dollar earner, with an enviable cash pile and profits. What the accounts didn't show was that overseas manufacturers took 11 per cent of the UK market in 1961 – and in 1975 it would be 28 per cent and still rising. It was into this storm that BSA was sailing, even if there wasn't a cloud on the horizon in 1951.

1951 was the year Jack Sangster joined the board of BSA following their acquisition of Triumph. He became chairman of BSA in 1956, following a series of board-room battles which ousted the previous chairman Sir Bernard Docker. Sangster then appointed Turner as chief executive of the Automotive Division (comprising BSA, Ariel, Triumph, Daimler and Car Bodies – makers of London taxicabs).

A key characteristic of BSA's directors – apart from Sangster and Turner – was their lack of knowledge of engineering, let alone the company's core motorcycle and gun businesses. There was a preference in British industry, including BSA, for managers and directors with wide general experience: 'good chaps' with the right education and background who were socially at ease in the boardroom. A grasp of law and accountancy was believed to be more important than the relevant technology, let alone a proven track record in the management of large manufacturing companies. This contrasted markedly with BSA's Japanese and European competitors, where engineers were routinely installed at boardroom level. It is probably fair to say that if British directors deigned to visit the shop floor – as Docker often did – they probably had no idea that the production line and engineering was so dated.

It has long been fashionable to knock British management from this era, an old boys' network recruited from public schools with a sense of entitlement born of Empire and financial security. But this is not borne out when looking elsewhere. Britain's service and financial sectors, civil service and more, were drawn from the same background, but were – and often remain – the envy of the world. What was lacking at BSA and similar businesses, as on the shop floor where an HND was often the highest qualification available, was training.

The first business school in the United States was established in 1881, and the first advanced degree in business – the Master of Science in Commerce, predecessor to the MBA (Master of Business Administration) – was offered in 1900. In Britain people were expected to learn on the job or show natural aptitude. However, where Britain was unique was that the engineering was also kept separate to the business: indeed, the business was often kept separate from the business, as this anecdote from Pat Slinn illustrates:

> *Wilf Harrison was export sales manager, and before that home sales and service manager. Wilf was a keen motorcyclist, and often took a bike from the end of the production line and rode it. One day he had been testing a Lightning Clubman and he got back to the factory at lunch time. He parked up the bike and went into the senior staff dining room still dressed in his Barbour suit, boots and such. He of course removed his riding gear before sitting down. Managing Director Lionel Jofeh happened to be in the dining room and saw Wilf in his riding gear, and told him that he did not wish to see his senior staff dressed in riding gear! He told him this in front of other people. I was in the normal staff dining room and this story was relayed immediately to us.*
>
> *Another story I heard was that Jofeh said he had never been into a motorcycle showroom in his life, and had no intention of doing so! I met Jofeh only twice, once when he came with a Home Office guy to see the BSA B40 Army bike that we had to put in the palatial BSA showroom, and once at an Earls Court motorcycle exhibition. I shook hands with him, but he never spoke to me.*

The separation of the eating places in the factory was again typical of the UK. We have seen how the Gold Star

Pat Slinn leaving as the factory's representative for the BSA international owners' club rally in Vienna, Austria. The passenger was Reg Reid, a senior engineer at Ariel and a one-time member of the Ariel display team. They are being seen off by Wilf Harrison, BSA export sales manager, and his assistant Peter Glover. The bike is a BSA Lightning Clubman with a Watsonian Monza sidecar.

and Experimental workshops often ate alone, separate from the factories canteen. Famously this contrasts with Honda's approach, where there was only one canteen and everybody, from the boardroom to the floor sweeper, was expected to eat together. 'The Old Man' – Soichiro Honda himself – could often be seen in his blue boiler suit queuing for something to eat.

The other contrast between *Honda San* and the BSA directors was that he saw himself as an engineer first, and brought in managers and money men to allow him to develop or reject ideas. He accepted he had no management experience, but he understood motorcyclists and their expectations, and how he might appeal to them. Honda thrived on offering the market what it wanted, and then turned to others to see how that might be done at a profit.

In Britain management looked first at ways to make a profit, and too often that was by keeping investment and development budgets under control. This wasn't to BSA directors' or shareholders' gain, since dividends were usually modest, if paid at all. What BSA did was accumulate a cash pile for acquisitions or downturns in the market, a feature of the see-saw uncertainty of post-war Britain. Contrast this with Sangster's preparedness to issue orders to upgrade specifications in the face of breakages, or Turner's sabbatical to visit Japan in 1960. He returned horrified at the march Japanese factories had stolen on Britain, and that Japan built around half a million machines a year compared to the UK's 140,000. Honda alone produced more motorcycles each day than the British motorcycle industry did in a week.

Yet Turner's concerns were dismissed by most of his fellow directors: Honda's arrival at the 1959 Isle of Man TT hadn't been met with foreboding, but rather greeted with wry amusement. Yes, their 125s had done well, but were inferior to the Italian equivalents from factories seemingly incapable of making a motorcycle of more than 500cc. This was the future, British 650s beloved of the true enthusiast. If the Italians and Japanese wanted to make small capacity commuters with a sporting edge, so much the better. Such lightweights would flush out true enthusiasts who would go on to buy a far more profitable British twin.

BSA's board concluded that the Japanese were a good thing, growing the market and thus the number of enthusiasts who would ultimately choose a heavyweight British motorcycle over the increasingly competitively priced family

The infamous 'Golden Zebra' 1955 Daimler DK400 Coupé.
ALF VAN BEEM

cars. After all, it was a strategy that was succeeding both in the UK and the US.

It is easy to mock Sir and Lady Bernard Docker for their naivety and extravagance with BSA's profits, perhaps most infamously with the 1955 Golden Zebra, a Daimler coupé based on the DK400 chassis. As with Lady Docker's previous company car, the Golden Zebra had gold plate where the standard car had chrome; an ivory dashboard; and zebra skin upholstery because Lady Docker decided that 'mink is too hot to sit on'. It was an extravagance too far. Sangster was elected by the board to replace Sir Bernard by a vote of six to three. Docker had already been ejected from the board of the Midland Bank for his conspicuous consumption, and would ironically soon run into financial difficulties. And yet both had their fans.

Pat Slinn was very much a new boy at BSA when the Dockers were forced out, but remembers female staff especially loving Lady Docker for her frequent forays on to the factory floor, and her insistence that things like the ladies' loos were kept up to scratch. Pat was kind enough to email an old colleague for me to see how his memories compared: 'I asked Michael Martin, who was Brian Martin's (BSA's competition manager) elder brother, what he knew about Jack Sangster. He was six or seven years in front of me at BSA. Here is his reply. It is certainly different to what I heard about Jack Sangster.'

J. Y. Sangster took over from Sir Bernard Docker in 1956 as Chairman of the BSA Group. I was a nineteen-year-old apprentice, so in a sense, what do I know?

What I remember is the reaction of the BSA shop-floor workers I was working alongside. They thought the world of Sir Bernard, and even more so of Lady Nora and her flighty behaviour. Whenever Sir Bernard appeared he was immediately recognized and was always 'encouraged' by the workers. The reverse applied to J. Y. Sangster, who was seen as the leader of the Docker ejecting coup, a faceless wonder to whom they could not relate. The BSA workers saw him as the 'enemy'.

The overall performance of the BSA Group went only one way after the transfer of power to J. Y. Sangster. Would it have done anyway? Despite the claims of the coup members one has to observe that during Sir Bernard's stewardship he brought in business contracts, particularly government military orders. If BSA had continued with Sir Bernard, would they have been making 'The Small Heath' rather than the Kalashnikov? Actually would we want that? When I worked in the Gun Model Room as a Small Heath apprentice there was work going on with advanced weapons including missile technology. Why did that end?

In the wider history BSA bought the Daimler Company just before World War II. At the time Dudley Docker wanted to purchase the largest car producer in the UK. This honour at the time was between Daimler and Rover. BSA purchased Daimler. Who was works manager at Rover? J. Y. Sangster!

Also the sales of Triumph and Ariel to BSA – were they astute deals or poisoned chalices?

Hindsight is a wonderful thing, and certainly BSA's military armaments business might have survived. Others have criticised the disposal of the tool-making business, pointing out that it remained highly profitable. Yet no British toolmaker from that era has survived, so the alternative timeline is unknowable. But all seem to agree that BSA started the post-war era with two priceless assets: dominance in the global motorcycle market, and a fantastic and fantastically loyal workforce at Small Heath. It seems that Docker at least appreciated and motivated the latter more than Sangster.

Sir Bernard died on 22 May 1978. Lady Docker died on 11 December 1983 and is buried in the churchyard of St James-the-Less in Stubbings, near Maidenhead, beside her husband. Jack Sangster retired as chairman of BSA in 1961, and died in Belgravia on 26 March 1977.

Cover of the BSA book, a seventy-six page A4 publication, celebrating the factory's centenary.
COLLECTION OF PAT SLINN

THE FUTURE LOOKS BRIGHT – BSA'S 100TH BIRTHDAY

Despite these machinations, on its centenary in 1961, an outsider might have thought BSA looked as if it had the world at its feet. A celebratory centenary book gifted to all employees wondered at the future of 'flying carpets' and the certainty of very similar manufacturing processes on BSA's second centenary in 2061. Few realized that the end was barely a decade away: certainly not anybody at BSA, who basked in the reflected glow of magnificent profits and much admired motorcycles, both reported on in the press with deserved admiration.

The hubris meant that BSA – along with much of the British manufacturing industry – was unprepared for the revolution that was coming. While many countries sought to protect their domestic manufacturers, especially as they grew from tentative post-war rebirth, the British were welcoming open trade in a remarkable turn of *laissez faire*. Chief among these was the Anglo-Japan agreement of 1962, which gave the Japanese almost unrestricted and immediate access to the UK market in return for little or nothing. Certainly not access to the Japanese market. This was seen as a diplomatic and generous offer to a broken nation that deserved help in rebuilding.

In reality Turner's well documented tour of the Japanese factories two years earlier should have served as a stark warning to British industry to remove the government's rose-tinted glasses. Instead the industry continued to wear their own pink-gin spectacles, believing the Japanese lightweights would help expand the market for motorcycles in general and large capacity British twins in particular.

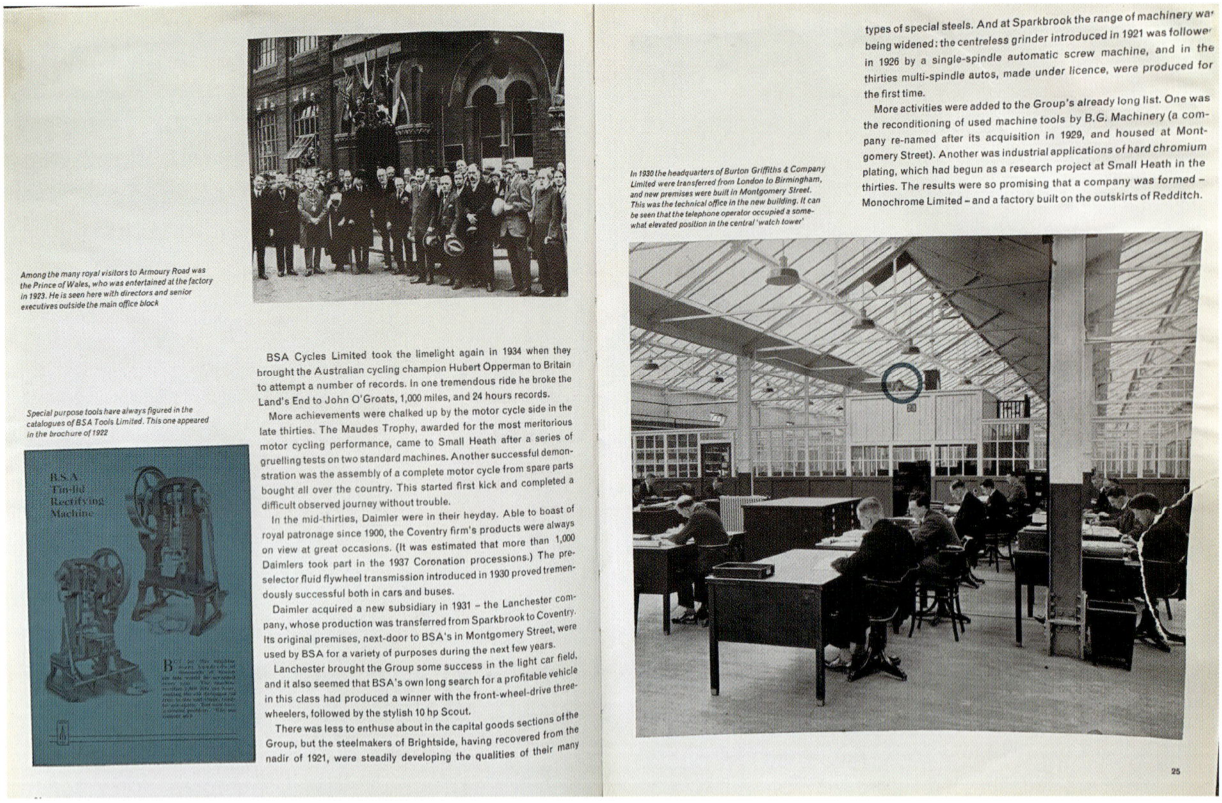

Among the many royal visitors to Armoury Road was the Prince of Wales, who was entertained at the factory in 1923. He is seen here with directors and senior executives outside the main office block

Special purpose tools have always figured in the catalogues of BSA Tools Limited. This one appeared in the brochure of 1922

BSA Cycles Limited took the limelight again in 1934 when they brought the Australian cycling champion Hubert Opperman to Britain to attempt a number of records. In one tremendous ride he broke the Land's End to John O'Groats, 1,000 miles, and 24 hours records.

More achievements were chalked up by the motor cycle side in the late thirties. The Maudes Trophy, awarded for the most meritorious motor cycling performance, came to Small Heath after a series of gruelling tests on two standard machines. Another successful demonstration was the assembly of a complete motor cycle from spare parts bought all over the country. This started first kick and completed a difficult observed journey without trouble.

In the mid-thirties, Daimler were in their heyday. Able to boast of royal patronage since 1900, the Coventry firm's products were always on view at great occasions. (It was estimated that more than 1,000 Daimlers took part in the 1937 Coronation processions.) The pre-selector fluid flywheel transmission introduced in 1930 proved tremendously successful both in cars and buses.

Daimler acquired a new subsidiary in 1931 – the Lanchester company, whose production was transferred from Sparkbrook to Coventry. Its original premises, next-door to BSA's in Montgomery Street, were used by BSA for a variety of purposes during the next few years.

Lanchester brought the Group some success in the light car field, and it also seemed that BSA's own long search for a profitable vehicle in this class had produced a winner with the front-wheel-drive three-wheelers, followed by the stylish 10 hp Scout.

There was less to enthuse about in the capital goods sections of the Group, but the steelmakers of Brightside, having recovered from the nadir of 1921, were steadily developing the qualities of their many types of special steels. And at Sparkbrook the range of machinery was being widened: the centreless grinder introduced in 1921 was followed in 1926 by a single-spindle automatic screw machine, and in the thirties multi-spindle autos, made under licence, were produced for the first time.

More activities were added to the Group's already long list. One was the reconditioning of used machine tools by B.G. Machinery (a company re-named after its acquisition in 1929, and housed at Montgomery Street). Another was industrial applications of hard chromium plating, which had begun as a research project at Small Heath in the thirties. The results were so promising that a company was formed – Monochrome Limited – and a factory built on the outskirts of Redditch.

In 1930 the headquarters of Burton Griffiths & Company Limited were transferred from London to Birmingham, and new premises were built in Montgomery Street. This was the technical office in the new building. It can be seen that the telephone operator occupied a somewhat elevated position in the central 'watch tower'

25

ABOVE: **Spread from the centenary book. Note the telephonist circled in her eyrie.** COLLECTION OF PAT SLINN

BELOW: **Spread from the centenary book, with eclectic examples of BSA's worldwide customer base.** COLLECTION OF PAT SLINN

THE WORLD ON TWO WHEELS

Left: To test the endurance of British motor cycles, three hardy riders took two BSA 650 cc twins with sidecars from London to the centre of the Sahara desert and back in 14 days

Right: One of the most advanced machines in the world is the Ariel Leader. It has the total enclosure and weather protection of the scooter with the performance and road-holding of the motor cycle

Above: Everyone – but everyone – rides motor cycles and it would seem that New Guinea natives are well up with the times!

Left: In the new countries of Africa the motor cycle is already popular. This Nigerian sailor is taking his girl friend for a spin on a BSA 250 Star

Right: In Australia many sheep farmers use motor cycles in the work of mustering their flocks. The sheep dogs love to ride on the tanks

70

71

The UK motorcycle market had already peaked in 1959, and BSA and Triumph especially turned once again to the US market to maintain sales and profitability. Yet Honda was already one step ahead of them, as JoMo (Johnson Motors), one of Triumph's brace of US distributors, discovered. Honda sales manager Hirobumi Nakamura agreed to meet the JoMo team, rather than the vice president they had invited. After introductions and smalltalk, JoMo team leader Bill Johnson asked how many motorcycles Honda expected to sell in the US. 'Five thousand' was the confident reply. At the time JoMo were selling some 2,500 motorcycles a year in their nineteen state western territories so, not unreasonably, Johnson responded that 5,000 a year 'was a lot of motorcycles'. 'No, 5,000 motorcycles a month' came the reply.

But a flabbergasted Johnson, like his British counterparts, soon got over his shock and came to the view that this would just grow the market, ultimately to the benefit of heavyweights such as the big Triumph and Harley-Davidson twins. Certainly there was no attempt to undermine or even compete with Honda through much of the 1960s, let alone stop them recruiting US dealers. Although it was against anti-trust laws to insist US dealers only stocked one marque, in practice it happened with distributors such as JoMo turning a blind eye if a dealer also stocked a small volume brand such as Ducati or Jawa, allowing them to claim adherence to the letter of the law, if not the spirit. And so Honda were allowed a bridgehead alongside the tiny European factories. Except Honda were soon flooding the showrooms.

The irony was that Honda had learnt from Triumph. They copied Triumph's showroom layouts, their warranties, and even their marketing strategy. Who can forget Honda encouraging everybody to take up motorcycling with their 'You Meet the Nicest People on a Honda' campaign? Yet a decade earlier US Triumph dealers had been specifically promised by Triumph that prospective buyers meant 'non-riders; the young men and women in school, the professional man, the businessman, the bank president, the church minister, the commuter, the sportsman, the serviceman… just to name a few'. The problem was that Honda was out to get those buyers too, and they were armed with resources and production capacities that BSA – indeed everybody else – could only dream of. Yet for now at least, even the Americans, to use one of their best known phrases, had to 'wake up and smell the coffee'.

Ironically the American Triumph importers were so impressed with the number of machines that Honda's new dealers were selling – many of them new to motorcycles – that exclusively Triumph franchises were torn up and new

The 1956 Honda Dream MF350: perhaps 200 were built to prove the factory's capabilities.

Honda's first big bike for the world market from 1965, the 450 Black Bomber.

free-for-all contracts awarded, often to these new wave Japanese dealers. Initially this brought a flood of orders, as the Honda dealers had the footfall from the smaller Hondas that quickly fed into sales for bigger British bikes. The scheme worked well until the CB450 Honda arrived – and even then buyers often stuck to Triumph, preferring to show off a 650 rather than a 450 that was just as quick. But Turner's belief that Honda were decades away from being able to build a 'big bike' should have been challenged at this stage, rather than await the rumour of a new 750. Even so, Honda's bridgehead into America was now unassailable.

BSA FIGHT BACK

Much credit is laid at the feet of Turner, but the more you dig, the less impressive the man is compared to his legend. His styling ideas were just that: ideas that his personal assistant, Jack Wickes, head of the design department, developed into the flowing lines of the classic Triumph profile. Indeed, Turner often introduced Wickes as 'my pencil'.

And what Turner referred to as the 'streamliners' – and everybody else called bathtubs – were especially unloved in the US. In the end, exasperated importers took to taking the TR6 – the 'naked' 650 with a conventional headlight, narrow mudguards and a generally sportier demeanour – and fitting a twin carburettor head, charging buyers $100 for the privilege. That the prototype Bonneville was presented as a streamliner wasn't the only disappointment to dealers: what they wanted was a faster TR6, not a twin carburettor T110.

The revered Bonneville – perhaps the most revered British parallel twin of them all – was also far behind BSA's equivalent, the A10, in specification. Triumph were still making lug and brazed frames, while BSA had introduced an all-welded steel tube duplex frame in 1954. The BSA frame was lighter and more rigid, though the Triumph engine was considered easier to tune. This led to many enterprising owners fitting Triumph engines in BSA frames, creating the TriBSA. That BSA didn't do this themselves shows how perverse was the relationship between the supposedly conjoined marques. But BSA never mastered styling the way Turner – sorry, Wickes – at Triumph did. And while BSAs were marketed as the sensible buy, Triumph was seen as the sportier brand. It was only when BSA started back on the road-racing trail that an attempt was made to change that, which brought the infighting into the open. But that's for a later chapter, as is how Triumph survived at Meri-

The BSA group's best seller, a 1960 Triumph Speed Twin in 'streamliner' guise. STEVE GLOVER

BELOW: **A modern interpretation of a TriBSA, a Triumph motor in a BSA frame.**

Variations on a theme: another TriBSA.

The 1964 Tiger Cub, the bike that would be the basis for BSA's unit-construction singles.
GRAHAM ROBERTSON

The 1953 Honda Dream 3E. The 145cc four-stroke single would have been a direct competitor to the BSA Bantam had it been shipped to the UK.

den, and why its survival is an insight as to how BSA might have lasted much longer than they did – perhaps even until today.

So it was Triumph that prospered, overtaking BSA during the 1960s as the best-selling marque in the US. Turner and Meriden had independence like no one else in BSA's portfolio, dating back to Sangster firing Turner in 1936 and offering him pretty much anything to return to his fold. Thereafter Sangster gave in on everything, from allowing Triumph's bombed factory in Coventry to be rebuilt miles away at Meriden, to allowing Turner to work half the year so that he could go gallivanting around the globe – and the US especially – for the other half. Turner was clearly a very gifted man, but also bloody minded, which rubbed off on the Meriden factory, Triumph surviving as a sit-in and then a co-op while BSA's staff went quietly into the night.

The irony is, as we will see at the end of this book, that the UK's head of Honda felt Meriden went in the direction he'd have gone in: salvation lay in retrenching, focusing on big, characterful bikes sold at a premium, just like Harley-Davidson. Meriden was killed in the end by not having the money to keep the Bonneville and production methods updated. BSA had plenty of cash until almost the end.

This contrasts with many observers claiming that the British motorcycle industry failed, including BSA (and thus Triumph), because they yielded the lower rungs of the motorcycle market. Boston Consulting Group (BCG) were commissioned by the Department of Industry to report in 1974 on the British industry's demise, and they pretty much laid the blame on what they called 'sector retreat': giving up each sector of the market until they were reliant on the big bikes alone. But this is patently not true of Triumph especially. There was the 350 bathtub, its bodywork intended to keep a rider clean, semi-automatic gearboxes, and various Tiger Cubs, all good entry-level proposals.

But BSA never had the resources to build on the scale of the Japanese, and so compete on price: realistically a 650 twin costs about the same to make as a 250 twin unless you can make them in the quantities the Japanese did. The truth is that, as the then head of Honda UK, Gerald Davison, has said to me: the British were too small to compete with the Japanese by the mid-1950s. And others – notably Ducati – who did try to offer a motorcycle in every sector, even in their protected home market, couldn't compete with the Japanese and eventually thrived only by building a premium product.

Anyway, BSA offered perhaps the most famous entry-level motorcycle that Britain has ever seen, the same bike that Harley-Davidson had used to try and build a bridgehead to the first-time rider: the DKW 125. Aka the Harley Hummer – and the BSA Bantam.

CHAPTER EIGHT

THE BANTAM

I first saw a BSA Bantam in August 1977, when a pillar-box red example pop-pop-popped up outside our house to deliver arrival instructions for my first full-time job – not as glamorous as it sounds, since this was the only way to be certain that an eighteen-year-old living in rural Wiltshire with a shared telephone line received anything. Even way back then the Bantam looked like a relic from another age, despite the last models having been registered just four years earlier. My telegram was in the rider's satchel rather than in a fibreglass top box or panniers, his comedy pudding-basin skull protector also looking as if it was a Pathé newsreel prop. If the Bantam hadn't been painted vivid scarlet I'd have sworn the whole thing took place in black and white.

Compared to my 1975 Honda 125S (which had replaced a 1959 C15), the Bantam looked what it was – a leftover from an era before Soichiro Honda had started school. My metallic blue Bikestyle full-face helmet was about the cheapest full-face helmet on the market, but a statement of intent to join the ranks of the big bike boys in the village – Bob with his Tango orange Laverda SFC 750 and Podge (really!) with his wayward Kawasaki Z1. I liked to think that a Japanese lightweight and the right riding kit said 'I'm on my way': the Bantam rider, with his despatch rider's coat and tight-lipped demeanour, might as well have had Pathé subtitle his clip 'I've got to do this, and it's faster than walking'!

Post Office Bantam D1 in Glasgow's Riverside Museum of Transport. The registration mark was issued in London in 1957. KIM TRAYNOR

Which is where these post-war lightweights all hailed from, unappreciated by my generation who had no idea how hard life had been. As I grew older I realized that for all the grumbling about the 1970s – strikes, power cuts, dizzying inflation and village life dying as mechanization replaced farm labour – just twenty years before our lives would have looked the stuff of dreams. The winter of 1963 saw villages cut off for six weeks, explaining why our elders lived in houses stuffed to the rafters with tinned food and garden sheds full of coal. Old rod-braked bikes were everywhere, often free to a good home, because the only work was several miles away and buses made their solitary appearances on Thursdays (market day in nearby Devizes) and Saturdays (for no obvious reason). The village was punctuated with forbidding cottages behind tall hedges where Mrs (or often Miss) Long-Forgotten lived alone, widowed or spinstered at an early age by a man who never returned from war.

It was this world that the Bantam was born into, a world where men seeking work had little beyond a demob suit and a half-remembered hero's welcome. Even the fact that the Bantam was essentially German was overlooked – or rather, not mentioned – a tactic perhaps borrowed from our royal family.

ORIGINS

In 1948, the year of its launch just as the dust settled on war, a Bantam wasn't a comedy skit, it was salvation, a way into work, rest and play, affordable (just, on Easy Terms), and genuinely capable of 100mpg (2.8ltr/100km). This was how post-war Britain got moving. The irony, of course, is that the Bantam wasn't British, or even initially for the British market: export or die, and all that. BSA's 'little rooster' was a revisited German DKW RT125, via a Danish engineer. In 1916 Jørgen Skafte Rasmussen founded a factory in Zschopau, Germany, to produce steam fittings. He tried building a steam-engined car, the Dampf Kraft Wagen ('steam-powered car'), the initials of which became the initials of his company. It failed to sell, but more conventional cars followed and were successful.

Skafte then made a two-stroke toy engine in 1919, called Des Knaben Wunsch – DKW again, but this time translating as 'the boy's wish'. Pleased with his efforts, Skafte gave an evolution of this motor two wheels and turned to selling these modest vehicles – scooters and motorcycles – with a move into production in the early 1920s. This led to another change of name, if not initials: DKW became Das Kleine Wunder ('the little wonder'), purveyors of very modest – and not

The 1950 DKW RT125W.

especially wonderful – two-wheelers that were cheap, utterly conventional, but dependable two-stroke transport. By the late 1920s DKW had become a serious player, building more than 40,000 powered two-wheelers in 1928 and becoming probably the biggest motorcycle manufacturer on earth.

By 1938 a supercharged DKW was good enough to win the Junior TT with Ewald Kluge, the reason Audi's sports car is called the TT: DKW was one of the four manufacturers subsumed into the Auto Union that begat Audi, and perhaps the most tenuous claim ever made by a car manufacturer. But later Deeks (as Brits tend to call them) had the four circles of the Auto Union on its badging, so the link is undeniable.

In 1929, a German engineer, Adolf Schnuerle, had developed the two-stroke's loop-scavenging system. With two intake ports, one on each side of the exhaust port, angled so that incoming fuel would flow to fill the entire combustion chamber, it would also push the charge from the previous combustion cycle into the exhaust port. This avoided the need for heavy deflector pistons and made the motor less prone to overheating, more powerful, and with reduced fuel consumption. No wonder it was part of the new DKW RT125's architecture, and that the RT125 (Reichs Typ, or National Model) was quick (a very relative term), reliable, and cheap to buy and run. The war came and went, but the RT125 remained in production.

Unfortunately at war's end DKW's Zschopau factory found itself on Russia's side of Germany's new big fence (soon to become an Iron Curtain), but some wise heads at DKW fled westwards and established a new workshop in Ingolstadt in Bavaria, north of Munich. As soon as the Allies gave the factory the green light, the reborn and relocated DKW began building the first post-war RT125W, suffixed to show it had been manufactured in the west. Its 123cc, long-stroke motor used an alloy head and an iron barrel and, crucially, a deflectorless piston. With a compression ratio of 5.9:1, claimed power was 4.75bhp at 5,000rpm. Primary chain drive was to a three-speed gearbox and chain final drive.

The design was good enough to survive most of the 1950s, and much longer in what became East Germany. MZ built them, as did IFA (Industrieverband Fahrzeugbau – Industrial Association for Vehicle Construction) in the old Horch factory (another of the Auto Union's) in Zwickau. The Russian RT125 replicas were sold as the M1A Moskva and K-125, while WFM of Poland also built a version (the SHL 125 and Sokół 125), which developed into the 125/175cc family that survived until 1985.

But the Ingolstadt DKW factory needn't have worried about keeping their design alive in the west. The Allies denied Germany any copyrights as part of war reparations, and so, keen to develop an entry-level range, Harley-Davidson's Hummer 125 was a Stateside take on the RT125W from 1955 to 1959. Meanwhile Yamaha, having re-established their production of musical instruments, decided to use facilities left over from wartime production to diversify into motorcycles. The Yamaha Motor Company was established in 1955 to make an improved RT125W as the first Yamaha motorcycle, the YA-1 'Red Dragonfly', from 1955 to 1958. But the version of the little Deek that we all remember is the one that BSA sold some 400,000 of – the Bantam.

THE FIRST BANTAMS

The unique thing about the Bantam compared to the other DKW RT clones is its right-foot gearshift, as was the norm on British motorcycles, but actually the exception across most of the world. The most plausible explanation is road camber: early roads tended to be particularly cambered (that is, raised in the centre with gutters at the sides to clear rainfall) so that, sitting at the roadside waiting to pull away to drive on the left, it was easier to steady the bike with the left foot and engage first gear with the right. If you drove on the right, as mostly everybody but the British did, the opposite was true. At first the Japanese manufacturers copied the British pattern – not only because some of their earlier bikes, like the Kawasaki W series, were based on British designs, but because they also drive on the left. But as they expanded they noted that most markets – and especially American riders – were used to a left-side shift, so, being an exporting nation, they adopted that pattern.

By the 1960s safety campaigner Ralph Nader decided that inexperienced or panicked riders might stamp on the gearshift when they wanted the back brake (still an important stopping aid back then), so persuaded the US government that standardization was needed. Harley-Davidson supported the move to their preferred left-side shift, which would mean their British competitors would have to spend money and time on linkages to accommodate the law, spoiling a gear shift that was generally much slicker than on Harley-Davidsons. But in post-war Britain a left-side gearshift was an anathema, and potentially a disincentive to stick with BSA when you graduated from a Bantam.

Nicely presented plunger-framed Bantam.

So the entire RT125's motor was redrawn as a perfect mirror image to ensure the gearshift was on the 'correct' side, and a home brewed – and never especially effective – electrical system added. The lighting was supplied by a 27W Wico-Pacy generator, direct electrics meaning no battery was needed, and that the engine would have to be running for the lights to work. Magneto ignition was supplied from the same unit. A small battery in the headlight shell allowed a pilot bulb to illuminate when parked, then still a legal requirement.

Better news was that the RT's girder forks were replaced with telescopic forks, although at the rear a single sprung saddle was all the suspension on offer, initially at least. This original Bantam, the D1, was released in October 1948, initially for export only, and continued in production for several years. It had a rigid rear end, a huge 'shovel' (resembling a digger shovel) front mudguard, a fishtail silencer, and was available only in 'Mist Green' – the same colour as the range-topping Sunbeam S7. The brakes were pressed-steel fittings, rather than the much better cast-iron items on later models.

The new Bantam sold for £60 plus tax (up to 33 per cent in Britain), when £100 a year was a typical annual income for a working man. This illustrates the danger of comparing prices over the years – with inflation, £60 in 1948 equates to around £2,000 now, but average full-time incomes are far more generous than the £3,500 that 1948's £100 is now equivalent to. So a new Bantam represented a huge chunk of most men's wages, yet even the next rung on BSA's ladder – the ancient side-valve 249cc C10 – was twice the price. According to Motor magazine in October 1948, the Ford Anglia was the cheapest car in Britain at around £300. And that would only do around 30mpg (9.4ltr/100km), and carried all the other costs associated with running a car – a carefully ridden Bantam would easily exceed 100mpg (2.8ltr/100km) at 40mph (65km/h).

On today's roads riding a Bantam alternates between being great fun and slightly terrifying. The early brakes are dreadful, especially compared to the Italian equivalents. The saddle is so low that six-footers will find their knees next to their elbows. And where most 1970s 125/175cc motorcycles can whip away from the lights with other traffic and cruise at 50 or 60mph (80 or 95km/h), even the later 175 Bantams can only manage 65mph (105km/h) flat out on a very good day, after a leisurely bout of acceleration. On back lanes, away from traffic, a 125 Bantam is perfectly entertaining, but in honesty initial acceleration is comparable to a decent bicycle – and the bicycle will have better brakes.

Yet on the move a Bantam is fun, fuss free and unpretentious. With its rigid rear end and softly sprung saddle, the D1 buzzes along comfortably enough at its claimed 40mph (64km/h) touring pace, and might hit 50mph (80km/h) with a tail wind. A head wind would be a different story – the

This period advertisement shows the wide Bantam range.

claimed 4.5bhp of the original D1 would grow to 7.4bhp for the D5 and D7, but when the 50cc sports mopeds of the early 1970s claimed almost that, phrases such as 'torque back-up' and 'unstressed' are best used to talk up the 125 Bantam.

For 1950, plunger rear suspension was optional but a debatable choice. BSA, like the entire British motorcycle industry, had taken forever to accept that rear suspension might be a good thing, and Moto Guzzi's pre-war arrangement was still a far better idea than plunger rear suspension. But plunger rear units could simply be added to a rigid frame, even if the Bantam's plungers didn't have oil seals and could require regreasing every week. It would be 1956 and concomitant with the dying gasps of the 148cc D3 (there was no D2, or indeed any even-numbered Bantams other than the D10 and D14) before a swinging arm was offered on a Bantam. All swinging-arm models had a longer silencer and shorter exhaust, since the new frame was unable to support the old fittings.

CAPACITY AND POWER INCREASE – BUT NOT BY MUCH

Post-1954 Bantams are easily spotted by their larger finned cylinder barrels and heads, improving cooling and allowing a capacity hike to 148cc. This was listed as a new model, the D3 Bantam Major. As well as the capacity upgrade, stronger front forks were fitted alongside a (slightly) beefier front brake. The larger capacity rocketed power from 4 to 4.9bhp – it doesn't sound much, but is a boost of over 20 per cent – although it sacrificed economy.

This tendency of the British to fettle – or bodge, if being cruel – rather than innovate would be in marked contrast to the Japanese. Despite their culture of *Kaizen* – continuous improvement, rather than innovation – the Japanese factories would be the groundbreakers. Gerald Davison, head of Honda UK, said to his Japanese engineers: 'If I gave you a blank sheet of paper it would still be blank in two weeks' time. If I gave you a set of plans you'd have improved them

Pat Slinn in the 1968 British team selection tests at Bordon. He is riding a 175 Bantam experimental ISDT bike, the engine built by BSA's two-stroke guru Michael Martin, brother of competition manager Brian. The front forks and wheel were BSA 441 Victor GP, the fuel tank Victor. The rest was standard BSA Bushman Bantam. COLLECTION OF PAT SLINN

It wasn't all hard graft: Pat Slinn (left) at a show with a Bantam and friend. COLLECTION OF PAT SLINN

by this afternoon.' And if you look at Yamaha's 'Bantam', the YA-1, you can see evidence of this. But Yamaha didn't stop there: their 125 single begat the 1957 YD-1 250 twin with a pressed-steel frame and McCandless-style rear suspension, a year before BSA's Ariel Leader. Ultimately this led to the TZ750 four, all tuned with technology stolen from MZ via Suzuki.

Yamaha, like the other Japanese factories, was in a hurry. 1957 would bring the Honda Benly, available as a 125 or 150cc four-stroke parallel twin. With an overhead camshaft, electric starter and up to 15bhp, the little Honda was given the ultimate bragging rights – and should have spurred every other manufacturer in the world into furious action – when the visually similar RC142 won Honda the 125cc 1959 Ultra Lightweight TT team prize. Instead the British talked of the folly of 4-valve heads, and dismissed the importance of the lightweight motorcycle market.

So BSA allowed the Bantam to thrum happily into 1958 as the 175cc D5, with 7.4bhp and a swinging arm as standard. The capacity boost meant another new cylinder barrel, most easily spotted by the slanted Monobloc carburettor. Even so, the D1 was left in the catalogue to bounce along on plungers until it was officially dropped in 1963, and the GPO might still have been buying them as late as 1968. The D5 – dubbed the 'Super Bantam' – raised top speed to almost 60mph (96km/h), the wheels shrank from 19 to 18in, while the tinware was painted Bayard Crimson or black and ivory. A larger two gallon (9ltr) tank allowed the D5 to match the range of the D1. Despite being almost identical to the D3, the D5 was only built in 1958, making it one of the rarest and most collectable of Bantams.

The following year came the D7 Super, restyled and reminiscent of the new C15, ready to convince buyers it wasn't as small or slow as it looked. And then it was a long wait for 1966 and another change in direction, with the Deluxe model joined by the cheaper D7 Silver. These models are distinguished by a new 1¾ gallon (8ltr) tank, with knee cut-outs. Apart from the obvious decrease in range, this had the effect of making the Bantam look slightly lanky and less like the C15, re-emphasizing that it was a manageable lightweight: whether that's a good or a bad thing is in the eye of the beholder. The 1950s 'fishtail' also disappeared from the end of the silencer, but more importantly, there were far more effective and long overdue cast-iron brake drums.

But it remained a Bantam (or a DKW RTW) at heart and was still a huge seller, with definite Swinging Sixties colours: Fuchsia Red and Sapphire Blue. Suspension and braking was upgraded again, even if the three-speed gearbox (still!) remained.

In 1967 BSA launched the D10, claiming a heady 10bhp and, with cubic capacity stretched as far as it could go, power was increased by raising compression from 7.4 to 8.65:1 and the addition of a larger concentric carburettor. A new Wico-Pacy alternator replaced the original after sixteen years of service, the reason the points shifted to the other side of the engine. A Bushman off-road model was offered with a high exhaust pipe and a new frame to justify the knobbly tyres. Mainly aimed at Australian sheep farmers, few were sold in the UK.

Another year brought another upgrade, and realistically the end of the road for the Bantam's development. The D14/4 ('4' for four speeds – at last) Supreme (1968–69), the Sports and Bushman (mainly exported, 1969–71) had minor tweaks – principally a compression ratio boost to 10:1 that gave 12.6bhp, finally comparable to Japanese singles, if not the twins. Along with a larger bore exhaust this gave a claimed 65–70mph (105–113km/h), belied by rather sober black or polychromatic blue tanks with chrome panels. More fitting to the times were the Sports' flamboyant red and the Bushman's orange, with high-level exhaust pipes. Only the Bushman retained the direct lighting, with all other models utilizing a coil and battery lighting system. The Supreme, Deluxe and Silver models remained three speed. Production of the D14 began late in 1967, early engine prefixes listed as D13, though this was never a model designation. With only about 600 made, perhaps they are the rarest Bantam of all.

The higher compression ratio made the bikes notoriously tricky to start and not especially economical – how the market for a basic 125 had changed over twenty years! The Supreme and Sports models changed the style of air filter, but the Bushman kept the pretty D10 pancake type.

The D14 only lasted a year, the subsequent and final D175 often also referred to as the B175. The most striking difference is the axially mounted spark-plug, a welcome relief for anyone who has ever tried to find top dead centre on a Bantam. The issue only took twenty years to address, in which time Suzuki had worked themselves up to the T125 Stinger: 15bhp, twin cylinders, five speeds, tachometer and indicators. BSA, along with the rest of the British motorcycle industry, thought that such things would never catch on.

CLASSIC BIKE RACING ON THE MOTOGIRO D'ITALIA

Racing Bantams became a surprise hit, trouncing more credible motorcycles in any number of scrambles events and even at the Isle of Man Ultra Lightweight TT. BSA hadn't expected this, but it didn't go unnoticed, the factory briefly offering both rigid and plunger bikes as competition models. Many changes were made to these, the most obvious being the upswept exhaust and a second hole in the cylinder for a decompressor. All competition and plunger Bantams were dropped in 1955, but there is one last famous competition Bantam floating around.

Hugo Wilson has been editor of both *Bike* and *Classic Bike* magazines, and is as much fun in person as he is in print. I got to know him over the week and 1,000 mile (1,600km) long (if you don't get lost) 2009 Motogiro. He was riding Classic Bike's Bantam project, a D1 with a much later 175cc motor. He was ever smiling, and great entertainment in the bar at the end of a long day, but goodness knows why – perhaps because he was getting paid to ride in achingly beautiful countryside.

But the thing that really shocked me was that his Bantam returned around 60mpg (4.7ltr/100km): less than my Ducati 450 Desmo, and that didn't use any oil. And the big single thumped out of the hairpin tornante with glee, where Hugo was sometimes down to first gear, discovering why the Italians call tiny (and tinny) two-strokes 'little donkeys': as they climb into the mountains you can hear the exhausts scream 'eeeee-awwww-eeee-awww' as the rider shifts between second and first. The only time the Bantam's speed got close to the Ducati's was on the mountain descents which, given the Bantam's brakes, wasn't especially welcome.

Hugo also seemed to have problems keeping the exhaust and silencer secure but, as already noted, the later systems weren't compatible with the plunger frame. And I think Hugo gave up on greasing the rear plungers because they looked mighty dry by the end of the week. But at least he rode on the final day's outing to Mugello, while I sat at the hotel nursing a failed regulator/rectifier. Given my hubris perhaps I should have been in charge of BSA.

1971 was the last year the Bantam was built, with BSA failing soon after. The Bantam might have been built to last forever (40,000 miles would be a good innings), but the Japanese two-strokes were sacrificing longevity for performance, which was, by the seventies, what the market was

The *Classic Bike* magazine Bantam project on the Motogiro d'Italia.

ABOVE: **Hugo Wilson, editor of *Classic Bike* and *Bike* magazines, with a Bantam on the Motogiro.**

The 1970 BSA D175: the penultimate BSA Bushman ever built.
KIERAN RICHARD MOLE

asking for. But today, at least from a classic owner's point of view, the Bantam's virtues are a good thing. It is easy to work on, and most parts are available and easy to fit, requiring few specialist skills. Apart from being the most numerous of classic motorcycles, the long production life of the Bantam – twenty-three years – its simplicity and general charm make it worthy of being classified as a classic British motorcycle. As long as you're never in a hurry – if you're a fan of the slow life – the Bantam might be just what you've been looking for.

CHAPTER NINE

SCRAMBLING TO WORLD CHAMPIONSHIPS

Born in 1934, by the winter of 1951 Jeff Smith's astounding early promise had factories practically queuing up for his signature on a works contract. He had won an ISDT gold medal aged just sixteen and, perhaps hubristically, declared his ambition to win both the ACU Trials and Scramblers Drivers' Stars, then effectively the UK's national championships – in fact they were arguably prototypes for the coming FIM world championships.

Jeff's initial commitment to Norton looked to be a mistake when the Bracebrook factory decided to abandon off-road competition in favour of road racing late in 1952. Faced with a stark choice between a free-of-charge Norton without factory support, or looking elsewhere for work, Jeff was left in an unenviable position. He would struggle to pay his way in professional competition after a lack lustre – by his standards – 1952: one win of a national trial and a 350 class win at Red Marley. This is how even the most glittering career starts can be forgotten and opportunities evaporate.

But, as most of us come to appreciate with age, it's not necessarily what you know, but who you know. Jeff's father, J. V. (Vincent) Smith knew BSA's competition manager Bert Perigo, and cornered him over a pint at the Birmingham motorcycle club. Perigo had first noticed Jeff 'at a Red Marley hill climb, an unknown sixteen-year-old on a clapped-out Norton, but he certainly had style. I made a mental note to keep an eye on him, but Norton got in first.' So despite BSA having a full team in Bill Nicholson, John Draper and Brian Martin, Perigo agreed to sell Jeff an ex-works 500 Gold Star for £100 with the promise of a full refund 'if he did well'. Jeff thought it a 'generous offer' and was photographed outside the Armoury Road factory with a big grin aboard the trial bike – registration number NOF 542, which Jeff recognized as factory rider Bill Nicholson's old motorcycle. He could clearly not have been happier.

Jeff Smith and BSA in action at the Dutch Grand Prix, 3 June 1962. DUTCH NATIONAL ARCHIVES, FOTOCOLLECTIE ALGEMEEN NEDERLANDS PERSBUREAU/HARRY POT

26 May 1962 at Noord-Brabant, Schijndel, in the Netherlands. The Gold Star heritage in the motor is clear. DUTCH NATIONAL ARCHIVES, FOTOCOLLECTIE ALGEMEEN NEDERLANDS PERSBUREAU/ HARRY POT

BELOW: **The bike BSA would build with their racing experience: the BSA 441 Victor Special. This is from 1968.** BONHAMS

The fruits of Jeff Smith and team's labours: Pat Slinn in the 1966 ISDT in Sweden aboard a factory-modified 441 Victor GP. Pat built the engine, and had no problems during the 1000-plus mile event, only needing to change the rear tyre and a throttle cable. It had an experimental Lucas capacitor discharge ignition system. This photo was taken during a special test on the third day of the trial. Pat was awarded a gold medal. COLLECTION OF PAT SLINN

Jeff and the big single gelled immediately, although he started the season with his father's faithful Norton 500T. He won the Premier award in two events that counted towards the 1953 ACU Trial Star championship. Taken under the wing of Bill Nicholson, with whom Jeff would travel to events and practices, he looked on course to deliver on his early promise. The British press were delighted to realize that Jeff was not the only new star on the block, with *Motorcycling* declaring the 'Terrible Trio' to be in a class of their own. Fans and reporters were in thrall to the battles fought in the fields of the United Kingdom between Jeff, Royal Enfield's John Brittain and AMC's Gordon Jackson. Brittain especially had been considered Smith's Nemesis, but he admitted that what made them the Terrible Trio was a shared 'never-say-die attitude'.

Jeff's early stamp of authority came in late February 1953 when he won the ironically named Triumph Cup in the Victory Trial. This was aboard his father's Norton (the clapped out one Perigo had noted?), with his BSA debut coming the following weekend in Ireland. Here Jeff claimed an impressive fourth place in the challenging Hurst Cup Trial, won by Gordon Jackson. This was followed immediately by an overnight journey with team mates John Brittain and David Tye to Cumbria (then Cumberland) for the Alan Trophy Trial in Sebergham, close to Penrith.

With Jackson absent, Smith took advantage in the race for the ACU Trial Drivers' Star chase with a narrow four-point win and his first taste of victory as a BSA rider. The season would continue in this nail-biting fashion until the all-important Scottish Six Days Trial (SSDT), where Jeff's Gold Star was skittled by a Canadian rider, leaving Jeff with a loss of twenty-six marks on the day. A lean mid-season followed, ending the season's points tally at eighty-two for Smith compared to ninety-nine for Jackson, and a full century for Brittain. But as was usually the case back then, not all results would count towards the championship, and Jeff took comfort in knowing that there were still three months to go until each rider's best ten results were totted up to decide who would be awarded the ACU's Drivers' Stars.

The system was complicated further by the ACU awarding points based on the number of competitors as well as results – a full ten points could be earned if there were over 100 competitors, but if there were ninety-something then nine points was the maximum available. When just thirty-three started the Reliance Trial, Brittain's win brought him only three points towards his annual tally, where Smith's win in the Streatham Trophy brought him ten because of the much larger field. While the ACU argued that winning against over a 100 other riders was harder than beating thirty-two, even Jeff felt the system was questionable – although, like his main competitors, he would plot to game the system. When the ACU announced a new season's events – of which there were many, often with a highly congested timetable by season's close – Jeff would sit down and think about where he could win against the largest field, and the logistics of travelling.

By the end of the 1953 Jeff's best ten results had accumulated ninety-three points, with Jackson on ninety and Brittain on eighty-eight. Jeff had his promised ACU Trials Drivers' Star, essentially making him national trials champion. He also had an extra £100 from Perigo, making good his promise of a full refund of his trials Gold Star's purchase price 'if he did well'.

Part of the BSA deal was that a Gold Star scrambler (what we would now call a motocrosser) would be made available, but Jeff and the BSA team were wise enough to keep these early cross-country races low key. Usually local to his home in Colne, Lancashire, Jeff took to the sport magnificently and came to prefer it to trials, in a large part because there seemed to be less luck involved, perhaps remembering the Canadian rider who ruined his chances in the SSDT. But BSA's star scrambles rider and future world champion could see there was trouble brewing in the company he was being asked to rely on:

> *For a weapons company put together by a group of gunsmiths in 1861, BSA had grown into a conglomerate of thirty companies in the UK and four subsidiaries overseas, manufacturing motorcycles, car bodies, specialized pumps, tools, special steels and guns. At the 100-year mark under the chairmanship of Jack Sangster, who retired that year, BSA had earned a record £3.5 million.*
>
> *The chairmanship was then handed over to Eric Turner, an accountant who came from the aircraft industry. Over the course of the next ten years Turner would oversee the downfall and eventual bankruptcy of this great enterprise. He was ably assisted by a management group, who except for a few standouts, lacked business sense, motorcycle engineering and imagination.*
>
> *Subtle changes began to be made in the management structure during 1962, and by 1963 it became*

Pat Slinn's own hybrid BSA, seen at the front of the book for a Classic Bike magazine photoshoot in its current yellow paintwork. COLLECTION OF PAT SLINN

known that Kinsey, an American business analytical group, would be looking at BSA with an eye to streamlining the design and manufacturing prowess of the company, and any non-complimentary or uneconomic parts of the group would be discontinued. This stuff was going on over the heads of the Competition Department. However, Brian [Martin], as competition manager, necessarily was drawn into some of the discussions of fund allocations and product planning.

Sometime during June or July of 1963 Brian told me he could not be certain that the Competition Shop would be operating in 1964, and that I should quietly begin to put together a stable of [alternatives to BSA works bikes, such as Husqvarna, Greeves, CZ and even Bianchi].

So while Smith got on quietly with his job at BSA and was pleased with progress on the new 421cc single, he also invested some £1,600 in a 250 Husqvarna and a Matchless 500 motor, together with the necessary parts to build a Metisse.

THE VANGUARD OF BSA'S COMPETITION SUCCESS

Jeff Smith would go on to become the world's leading motocross racers of the 1950s and 1960s. He won the 500cc World Motocross Championship in 1964 and 1965 riding for BSA. He was also a six-time member of the winning British Motocross des Nations team. Equally significant was Smith's success in his eleven ISDTs, earning a gold award on eight occasions.

Smith's transition from trials to motocross sensation looked – to those not following his career – like overnight success. He had raced only a few local scrambling events when BSA asked him if he would like to enter the Dutch Motocross Grand Prix as part of the factory team in 1954. Expectations were modest, given that this was simply the first rung on the ladder and he was joining an already impressive BSA team. Of course the young Smith jumped at the chance, and then stunned the motocross establishment by winning. Unsurprisingly he remembers it well: 'Fortunately it rained like mad, so it was really more of a trial than a motocross. When I got back, the head of BSA racing told me that perhaps they should let me race in more scrambles and motocross events.'

Within weeks of returning to England, he won the prestigious Experts Grand National scrambles meeting. In 1955 he

The road-going version of the big 441cc single, the B44 Shooting Star, aka the Victor Roadster, built from 1966 to 1970. TR001

won the British Grand Prix – and a long motocross career at world championship level was up and running. Smith competed from the mid-1950s to the late 1960s, racing in front of some of the largest crowds ever to witness motocross grands prix. 'The biggest crowd I raced in front of was in Leningrad [now St Petersburg in Russia] in about 1962, when there were over 100,000 people watching. In Prague the next year there were over 90,000 spectators. I mean, that's a very big crowd.' Jeff Smith can be a master of understatement.

Part of his mastery was looking after his machine during a race at a time when breakdowns were a constant threat. Motocross motorcycles were not the robust, usually trouble-free machines they became as the Japanese took over the sport. Many a rider lost races and even championships due to 'mechanicals' – a euphemism for machinery breaking – but Smith's factory BSAs had an enviable finishing record.

What made this especially impressive was that the four-stroke singles of the time were being pushed closer and closer to their limits by the arrival of lighter and more powerful two-stroke motors. During his first 500cc Motocross World Championship-winning campaign in 1964, Smith rode his BSA B40 (which had started in production form with 343cc, soon punched out to 421cc) to six victories in thirteen rounds, never finishing off the podium. He won the title by a narrow margin over Swede Rolf Tibblin, who'd won the world titles in 1962 and 1963. The championship wasn't decided until the final race, and it almost came as a relief to

The 1964 Dutch Grand Prix in Sint Antons, Jeff Smith in the lead again. Note the motor is now unit construction.
DUTCH NATIONAL ARCHIVES, FOTOCOLLECTIE ALGEMEEN NEDERLANDS PERSBUREAU/HARRY POT

Smith: 'By then I was thirty, and I have to say that I thought I was never going to win the world championship. Obviously, experience and an excellent machine came together at just the right moment, and I managed to win the championship.'

In 1965, Smith was so dominant that by halfway through the season he'd already clinched his second world championship. With the title secured, BSA asked Smith to abandon his works bike and try to win a grand prix on a stock model, just like the ones in the showrooms. 'I have to admit I couldn't do it,' Smith recalls. 'I tried, and the best I did was finish sixth in the East German Grand Prix. So I earned one world championship point on the standard machine.'

The 1965 title proved to be the swansong for the thundering four-stroke singles. The following year East German star Paul Friedrichs won the first of three consecutive 500cc world titles on CZ two-strokes. Even so, BSA and Smith didn't give up, and wheeled out something special for 1966:

> *BSA very much wanted me to win a third consecutive championship, promising to build the most advanced motocross bike ever assembled. But then things went awry because not all of the engineers were motorcycle engineers, and somehow the whole project got out of hand. We had a motorcycle that was basically made out of titanium, dubbed 'The Titan' by the motorcycling press.*
>
> *Too many cooks spoil the broth, I'm afraid, and unfortunately the machine... well, it eventually became successful as the B50, but it took four years. So we had the whole year in 1966 when we had so many problems, really developing the machine at the grand prix races, and that's not the way you should do it.*

In all, Jeff Smith won nine British championships in addition to the two world titles. He then moved to the United States in 1970, and won the first two Trans-AM races ever held, the first in La Rue, Ohio and the next in New Berlin, New York. He briefly returned to the UK for a visit to Buckingham Palace in 1970, where he was awarded Member of the British Empire (MBE) for his services to motorcycling.

After retiring from full-time competition, Smith helped develop Can-Am's motocross machines in the mid-1970s. He then went on to head up the American Historic Racing Motorcycle Association (AHRMA) in the 1990s, and directed that sanctioning body through a time of rapid growth when the organization went from around 800 members to over 5,000. He retired from his leadership position of the AHRMA in 1999.

Smith and his wife Irene (sister of another famous British racer, John Draper) retired to Wisconsin, where they live with daughter Chris, who still runs the motor sport magazine and book business Jeff founded. Their son and daughter also became vintage motocross racing champs, and even into his seventies, Smith still won various vintage championships on 1960s-era machines such as his beloved BSA.

At the time of writing he is still happy and healthy, with a wicked sense of humour that he shared with his late sparring partner and friend Dave Bickers. Tales of their high jinks, especially behind the Iron Curtain, are a reminder of just how different motorcycle racing is today, and how versatile riders needed to be.

Two other BSA singles riders also deserve mention: Fred Rist and Arthur Lampkin.

FRED RIST

There was an embarrassment of riches in the BSA team, although Jeff Smith deserves singling out for his world championships. The riders in the 1952 Maudes Trophy challenge have already been celebrated and included Fred Rist, who would become a legendary sand racer post war. But perhaps his most defining moment was during the 1939 ISDT in Austria. The army team had secured three works bikes for their nine riders from each of three factories: Norton, Matchless and BSA. The latter were led by Fred Rist, with his sergeant rank, Corporal A. C. 'Paddy' Doyle and Private Jackie Wood. They were accompanied by Bert Perigo and reserve rider Joe Acheson, with 500 Gold Stars registered in 1938.

They looked to have the event won until Hitler ordered the invasion of Poland that would precipitate Britain going to war with Germany. All the army riders therefore fled on the final day of the ISDT, riding across Switzerland and France to return to England. They barely made the ferry before war was declared on 3 September, just escaping becoming POWs before Britain had fired a bullet. As some have written, this was the real 'Great Escape'.

Post war, Rist continued to ride for BSA's ISDT team and was captain on – of course – a Gold Star in 1950. But he drifted, and eventually retired, from competition to concentrate on his motorcycle business in Neath, Glamorgan. After

The Royal Tank Corps team of Paddy Doyle (left) Fred Rist (centre) and Jackie Wood with reserve Joe Acheson (left rear) on the 1938-registered Gold Stars used for practice prior to the 1939 International Six Days Trial in Austria. Picture taken at the BSA factory, with Bert Perrigo.

Newspaper cutting reporting on Fred Rist and fellow 1939 ISDT team members. UNKNOWN PUBLICATION

all, there is some spectacular off-road riding to be had in that part of Wales, and anybody drawn to sand racing would want to live close to the legendary Pendine Sands.

ARTHUR LAMPKIN

Arthur Lampkin was born in Kent, but his father moved the family to Silsden in West Yorkshire in 1941. Arthur was riding his father's BSA before he was old enough to have a licence, and bought his own motorcycle with money earned from his paper round. At eighteen he won the British trials national championship, joining the BSA factory team alongside his brother Alan as the 1960s dawned: he would become known as 'Mr BSA' to fans. Along with Dave Bickers and Jeff Smith, the Lampkins were part of a crowd that dominated scrambling and then motocross in a golden era. Arthur took the runner-up spot behind Bickers in the 1961 European motocross championships, then for 1962, with the series upgraded to world championship status for the first time, he finished the year in third place behind Torsten Hallman and Jeff Smith. He was also part of the British teams that won the Trophée des Nations in 1961 and 1962, as well as the 1965 Motocross des Nations.

The Motocross Des Nations 1967 at Markelo, the Netherlands. Arthur Lampkin is #4 on his BSA. Also pictured are Gunars Draugs (CZ, 11), Vic Eastwood (BSA, 3), Åke Jonsson (Husqvarna, 8), Torsten Hallman (Husqvarna, 6).
DUTCH NATIONAL ARCHIVES, FOTOCOLLECTIE ALGEMEEN NEDERLANDS PERSBUREAU/ERIC KOCH

In a full and challenging calendar that seems unimaginable today, Lampkin competed in plenty of other off-road motorcycle competitions, winning the prestigious 1963 SSDT and the Scott Trial in 1960, 1961 and 1965. In international enduro events, representing Great Britain, he earned a gold medal in the 1966 ISDT in Sweden. After retiring from competition, Lampkin took over his father's engineering business. His nephew, Martin Lampkin's son Dougie, would become twelve-time trials world champion.

A RETURN TO ROAD RACING – THE MC1

The BSA MC1 is another of those 'if onlys' that are scattered through the British motorcycle industry's history, like old confetti at a long-forgotten wedding. With a near horizontal cylinder, it was developed almost in parallel with Norton's F (flat) single that was part evolution of the Manx, part recognition that Moto Guzzi's horizontal singles were the only things that could keep the MV and Gilera multis in sight. When Hopwood moved from Norton to BSA in May 1948 he persuaded Hele to follow him – as he would when they returned to Norton in 1955.

By 1950 Hopwood, now BSA's chief designer, had sketched out a 250cc single, aiming to win the Junior TT and lay the foundations for a new generation of BSA sports motorcycles. He passed his drawings to Hele, charging him with bringing the MC1 project to fruition.

Hele was perhaps the British motorcycle industry's greatest engineer, the only other contender being Val Page. While Page was the quiet genius behind Turner's ego, Hele fulfilled a similar role for Hopwood. While Hopwood liked to portray Hele as a favoured son or apprentice, Hele neither liked nor respected Hopwood. Having been passed Hopwood's design for a BSA single-cylinder racer to complete, Hele's remarks later in life said it all:

> *Hopwood was a very stylish designer, but unfortunately his engines would sometimes not run. Bert's original design for the BSA MC1 racer could not have run, because the chain-driven ohc camshaft would not have been able to open the valves. This is not a minor mistake – indeed it had a quite serious set-back, in so far as the valves were the wrong way round and so would not open. The radial valves couldn't work because they got entangled. But it was very stylish.*

THE MC1

Year: 1954
Displacement: 248.5cc
Bore/stroke: 70 x 64.5mm
Compression ratio: 10.1:1
Engine type: Four-stroke air-cooled dohc horizontal single with bevel gear camshaft drive, 4 radial valves and external flywheel
Carburation: Two Amal carburettors
Ignition system: Magneto
Claimed power: 34bhp at 10,250rpm (at gearbox sprocket)
Transmission: Multiplate dry clutch, four speed Burman racing gearbox. Primary and final drive by chain
Brakes: Single leading shoe drum front and rear
Chassis: Tubular double cradle frame, leading-link front suspension, Girling monoshock rear suspension
Weight: 248lb/112kg
Top speed: 105–110mph (169–177km/h)

By the time Hele had finished with the MC1 it was arguably the most advanced road racer on earth. Twin carburettors fed 4 radial valves controlled by bevel-driven double-overhead camshafts (dohc). Hopwood's square 68 x 68mm bore and stroke were replaced by short stroke and free-revving 70 x 64.5mm dimensions. An external flywheel mimicked Moto Guzzi for good reason, minimizing internal friction and allowing a smaller, stronger crankcase. The chassis was low slung, the MC1 smaller than any 250 had the right to be, despite a TT-friendly 7gal (32ltr) fuel tank. The steering head layout for the leading-link front forks was unconventional but kept frontal area minimal. The monoshock rear suspension was twenty years ahead of its time.

Three engines were built, and a prototype lapped the Motor Industry Research Association's (MIRA) banked test track at 104mph (167km/h) without streamlining. When reigning 500cc champion Geoff Duke showed an interest, he was offered a ride over the winter of 1954. His upbeat comments and the rumour that he had broken Oulton Park's lap record – although Duke said he was two seconds shy – led to fevered speculation that BSA would make a long-overdue return to road racing. That BSA had taken the first five places at Daytona that year – the third spot by Tommy McDermott on a Gold Star – further fuelled talk of a victori-

Pat Slinn with the MC1 in Sammy Miller's museum.

Detail of the MC1's motor.

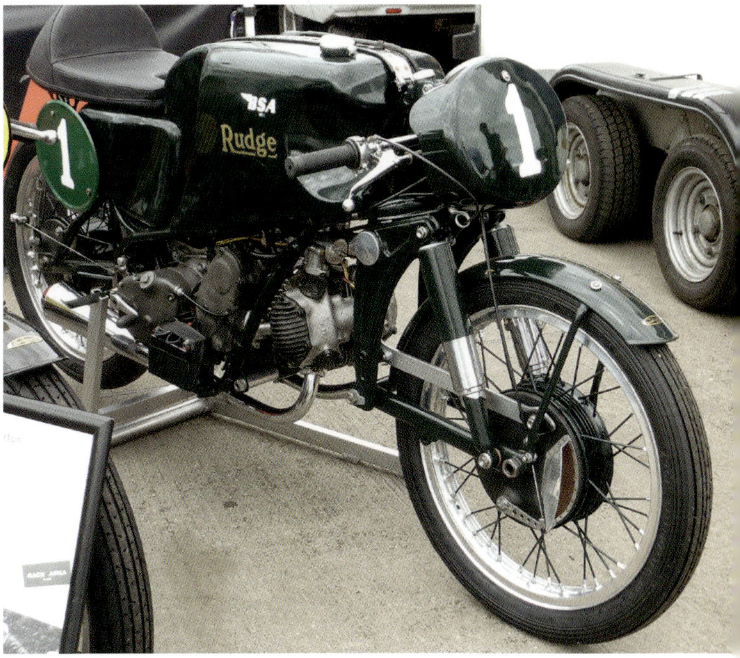

Another MC1, badged 'Rudge' as Hopwood intended for its debut race.

ous TT comeback to finally erasing the pain of BSA's 1921 TT humiliation.

Duke's criticism, apart from complaining of a misfire, was reserved for the front brake and Burman four-speed gearbox – he wanted a fifth ratio, especially given that the MC1 had yet to be fitted with streamlining. The misfire was due to the magneto struggling with the rapid pick-up of the rev-hungry engine; single shoe brakes were taking weight saving too far; and BSA could easily build their own gearbox. So these were failings simple enough to remedy, but mindful of the risk of failure, Hopwood entered the MC1 as a Rudge for its debut race. BSA still owned the defunct Rudge name, and the MC1's radial valves reflected that heritage. Geoff Duke would enter it at the TT as a GDS – Geoff Duke Special – so that any teething difficulties would not tarnish BSA's reputation. But once a proven winner, Hopwood hoped the MC1 would be reborn as a next-generation BSA Gold Star, with a road-going version following. How such a machine might be sold with a realistic price tag is not recorded, although it is hypothetical because it never happened.

The story goes that the board, led by James Leek, asked Hopwood and Hele if they could guarantee a win first time out – and of course they couldn't. Internal politics also railed against anything that might divert funds from the off-road competition department. So the MC1 was summarily dismissed as a blind alley, and it would be another five years before a new BSA 250 was on the cards. Where Hopwood and Hele had once hoped this would be based on the MC1 and bask in the glory of TT wins, instead we got the C15. Little wonder that by then the pair had returned to Norton.

CHAPTER TEN

PART OF THE UNION 1: MODERNIZING THE SINGLES

It is hard to believe that Jeff Smith's winning BSA motorcycles had their roots in perhaps one of the most unimpressive motorcycles ever built. The C15 was for a rider on a budget, but perhaps more importantly with an eye on changes to UK legislation that would limit new riders (albeit still allowed a provisional licence at sixteen years old) to a motorcycle with no more than 250cc from 1960, and a requirement to display 'L' (learner) plates until the perfunctory test was passed.

Quite why the British motorcycle industry took so long to adopt unit construction – that is, the gearbox within the crankcase rather than as a separate bolted-on unit – is a mystery. While it is true that gearbox teeth break down oil

A 1960 C15, obviously restored but as it might have been when new, although the mirror is modern. MICK

more quickly than bearings, and that in unit construction the oil is shared between the gearbox and the crankshaft and conrod bearings, necessitating regular oil changes, otherwise the advantages of unit construction are compelling: stronger engine and gearbox cases; less wear and adjustment to the primary drive; better oil tightness; and a more compact and easy to package power train. The Italians went to unit construction almost from the start, except for the factories that bought in engines – and therein probably lies the truth: it was easy to buy in engines and gearboxes and call yourself a motorcycle factory – designing and building a motor in house was far trickier.

Yet BSA's huge factories made their own nuts and bolts, never mind gearboxes. It was probably an attitude – accepting the status quo – that would not survive the arrival of Japanese machines. These not only had unit construction, but also horizontally rather than vertically split crankcases that simplified assembly and reduced the chance of oil leaks. Internally BSA's C15 was still a pre-unit motor at heart, although one that was now more closely related to the Tiger Cub, itself derived from the 1953 150 Terrier.

Edward Turner had become head of the BSA automotive division following Jack Sangster's wrestling of BSA's chairmanship from Sir Bernard Docker in 1956, and knew he needed to come up with a 250 that complied with the change in the driving licence rules fairly promptly. Turner had been a fan of unit construction for a while and, by combining the best of the Triumph Cub and BSA C11, he could come up with what looked like a completely new model in short order and at minimal cost. The C15 Star was thus the first true unit-construction BSA and thankfully proved more reliable – if not as much as it should have done – and economical than its predecessor.

The vertically split crankcase and gearbox castings still needed to be matched and drilled so that the crank and gearbox aligned, rather than being dropped into a pre-prepared bottom half of a horizontally split crankcase. The C15's pressed-up crank had a ball race bearing on the drive side, and plain bushes on the timing side and big end. From here, a layshaft below the mainshaft took power to the gearbox, not unlike the old C12. The alternator and oil pump ran off a cam-driven shaft, and on the right-hand side the timing camshaft ran above the crank to control the overhead valves via alloy pushrods. A 375 Amal carburettor with a bore of just 7/8in (22.2mm) gave great fuel economy but only a claimed 15bhp: realistically this meant a cruising speed of around 50mph (80km/h), but potentially 70mpg (4ltr/100km).

Gradually the lack of ambition BSA showed with the C15 would lead to it being lumped into what motorcyclists called the 'grey porridge' category: it did the job, but without much joy. On the upside it was light and, with an all-new chassis and poised on mere 17in wheels, easy for a new rider to handle. It was also a shame that the styling hinted more at the Bantam and A7 it shared showrooms with, rather than the Triumph twins that were wooing America.

The C15's dull styling, compared to what Turner (or rather Jack Wickes) was able to pen, was probably linked to grumbles in the boardroom about rationalization between models being long overdue. Indeed, by 1961 Turner was under pressure to retire, and was anyway more involved with the car side of the business, notably the V8 motor in the Daimler Dart. And it was also true that in the UK the C15 faced little competition, both the Royal Enfield 250 Crusader and Norton Jubilee twin suffering from reputations for oil leaks and poor reliability, with the Norton offering hardly any more power than the C15 – 16bhp versus 15bhp – despite weighing rather more. Even Triumph's 350 twin only claimed 18.5bhp, almost laughable in the face of Honda's CB77 305cc Super Hawk's 28bhp.

Honda's 250 version, the CB72, might have given less, but it was still far better specified. Author Aaron Frank called these 'the first modern Japanese motorcycles', and their credibility was assured when Elvis Presley rode a CB77 in the film *Roustabout*. Customer loyalty, styling and credibility kept customers coming back to the British bikes, but with BSA's main board all thinking of retirement rather than where the business might be in a decade or more, the end was in sight for anyone who cared to look for it.

And the C15 didn't have a trouble-free introduction, despite being the continuation of a line, rather than the all-new model BSA liked to claim. The motor needed careful assembly and maintenance if it wasn't to suffer from oil leaks, gearbox gremlins, valve-train issues and even big-end failures. Clutch adjustment was needed regularly and, almost inevitably the electrics too often didn't work as riders hoped. Initially the car-style contact-breaker housing protruded at the rear of the cylinder above the gearbox, but it was later relocated to the right-side crankcase. Again, BSA, like its cohorts, hoped gradual tweaks would keep showrooms busy.

The frame was still lug and brazed, despite BSA introducing an all-welded steel tube duplex frame in 1954 for

A 1965 BSA C15 Sport Star SS80. STEVE GLOVER

its twins. This was pre-World War I technology that had long been surpassed by welded steel tubes, for light weight and strength, or by pressed steel, for cost on lightweights, arguably pioneered by market leaders NSU and copied by Honda, Soichiro himself being a huge admirer of the German machines. The nascent European Economic Community was still tricky to deal with, but Honda were about to have untrammelled access to the UK market with the 1962 Anglo-Japan agreement. BSA could easily have gone to pressed steel, with the Austin works at Longbridge nearby or indeed their own facilities at Daimler. Perhaps they were worried about competing with the Ariel 250s, but for whatever reason, BSA entered the Swinging Sixties with the C15, perhaps the motorcycle to be expected when you ask old men what sixteen-year-olds want.

So predictably, despite the failing big ends and slipping clutch, those sixteen-year-olds demanded more performance than the C15 could offer. BSA's answer was the SS80, the name hinting at the claimed top speed. The C15's overwhelmed plain main bearing and iron crankshaft were replaced with caged rollers and steel, but by the time compression was raised to 10:1, bigger valves and carburettor added and a higher lift camshaft installed, reliability went backwards. A drop to 8.75:1 compression followed and, more worryingly, the SS80 still looked more ride-to-work than ride-to-win.

The unimaginative styling of the C15 reflected the desire to offend no one. Not only was the C15 meant to appeal to sixteen-year-olds, the claimed huge cost of retooling to build this new venture meant that it was also aimed at ride-to-work and touring types to replace the B31 in BSA's line-up. Trying to broaden the C15's appeal, the 67mm bore was taken out to 79mm, creating the 1961 343cc B40, an enlarged version of the C15 that failed to address many of the 250's shortcomings. Certainly it was torquier and more pleasant to ride, but beyond that added nothing to the ownership experience. So, as with the C15 80SS, there followed a B40 SS90 sports model, introduced in 1962. This promised 90mph (145km/h) from a bigger inlet valve, raised compression, hotter camshaft, larger carburettor and close-ratio gearbox. For spotters the SS90 was identified by bright red paintwork, chrome-panelled fuel tank and mudguards: be still, my beating heart.

This, incidentally, was very different to the 'B40' that Jeff Smith was riding, and really a mule that competition manager Brian Martin could use as a work in progress. It also tied the works bikes to a production model for homologation purposes, allowing competition models to be sold. So the 1960 B40 took the C15's already overworked big end, gearbox and clutch and, in an attempt to rescue reliability, BSA reduced compression to 7:1. A big jump in weight, from the C15's 280lb (127kg) to 384lb (178kg), brought brakes up from 6in to 7in and wheels to 20in and 18in front and rear respectively, supported by a welded, Victor-style frame. A B40 feels much more relaxed and torquey to ride than a C15, despite outright power increasing from 15 to 20bhp.

None of this appealed much to private buyers, who saw through BSA's attempt to save on costs with little concern for innovation or improving reliability. Only a Ministry of Defence order for 2,000 B40WDs saved the project, with other government orders following. These bikes introduced a stronger roller and ball-race bottom end with a roller big end. In addition, according to Pat Slinn who was developing the C15 motor for ISDTs and such:

ABOVE RIGHT: **Working on the BSA B40 ISDT British Army bike.**
COLLECTION OF PAT SLINN

RIGHT: **Military B40.**
ALF VAN BEEM

The ratios fitted to the original Army B40s had a low first and second gear, so were acceptable for trials use. However, some bikes were specified by the MoD for long-distance convoy work and the like, so they simply had standard C15/B40 gearboxes. Even so, the permutations and specifications for the military bikes and engines were wide, being different for the British army, military police, Navy and Air Force, and customs and excise to name a few that I can remember. There were specifications for the Danish, Swedish and Australian armies: the Australians actually used some of theirs in Vietnam during the war! At least two were sent for US military evaluation to BSA Incorporated on the West coast of the States.

There were also surprisingly competent off-road versions of the 250, the C15 Trial and C15S Scrambler, which sold well in the afterglow of Jeff Smith's achievements. These were unquestionably the best of the C15s. The C15T had a higher ground clearance frame with a sump bash plate, revised gear ratios and a high level exhaust. The all-alloy motor was tuned for trials use, and an optional lighting kit allowed it to be road legal. The C15T proved competitive at club, and even national level in the right hands, and remained unchanged until 1965.

The C15S motocross version was built between 1959 and 1965. As with the trials version, the C15S saved the weight of a battery through a notoriously unreliable 'energy transfer' system, with the timing and points gap requiring far too much precision for an off-road competition motorcycle. The C15S was unsilenced and had strengthened fork springs with rubber fork gaiters.

In 1964 and 1965 the overbored BSA C15T 'Trials Cat' ridden by Jeff Smith won the 500cc World Motocross Championship, the campaigns allowing development of the 441cc BSA Victor Scrambler.

And finally, in 1963, the C15 gained a welded frame.

A 1961 BSA C15T trials machine. CRAIG HOWELL

THE C15

Year: 1965 (model available 1960–1967)
Displacement: 247cc
Bore/stroke: 67 x 70mm
Compression ratio: 7.25:1
Engine type: Four-stroke overhead-valve vertical single
Carburation: 7/8in (22.2mm) 375 Amal carburettor
Ignition system: Alternator
Claimed power: 15bhp
Transmission: Multiplate wet clutch, four-speed unit-construction gearbox. Primary and final drive by chain
Brakes: 6in single leading shoe drum front and rear
Wheels: 17in front and rear
Chassis: Telescopic front forks, twin shock absorber rear swinging arm, half duplex frame
Weight: 280lb/127kg
Top speed: 70mph (113km/h)

TO THE VICTOR, THE SPOILS

The story goes that BSA's competition manager Brian Martin took a C15 from the production line, removed the lights, and added bigger wheels, an alloy tank and upswept exhaust. Thus armed, Jeff Smith and Arthur Lampkin finished second in the 250cc European Motocross Championship over the next two years. Pat Slinn, who worked in BSA's experimental department, as his father had before him, laughs at this notion that the works bikes were based on C15 motors pulled from the production line:

> *They were much more special than that. The crankcases might have been based on the C15's but they were always being developed, made stronger, stud spacings changed for bigger barrels. And there were a lot more people than Brian and Smithy who deserve credit for BSA's success. Without John Thicken especially there would have been no world championships. He was just such a good engine builder.*

Jeff Smith agreed, writing in *Motor Cyclist Illustrated* that 'Our Welsh wizard, John Thicken, the man responsible for the engines, has spent a lot of time on the twin problems of reliability and performance. We believe he has struck a fine balance between the two.'

Smith's winning BSA became unrecognizable to C15 owners. The cheap-to-make swan-neck headstock of the C15's frame was immediately discontinued, replaced by a much more robust and seriously braced item that would become a key part of the all-new Victor Enduro/Roadster's frame. Every aspect of the brakes was revisited. And in truth, the B40 was much closer to the Victor's starting point than the C15: it was just that BSA needed the publicity to sell C15s.

Between early 1961 and Good Friday 1962 the B40 engine was developed into a 421cc competition version, creating the motorcycle that would take the world championship. The chassis was already of oil-in-the-frame design, plus a small supplementary tank below the airbox. The bike weighed just 228lb (103kg). The 'titanium' bike (dubbed 'Titan' by the press, but suffering from trying too hard to lose weight) tipped the scales at a featherweight 202lb (93kg) in an attempt to thwart the two-strokes.

For 1966 BSA had the 441cc B44 Shooting Star (Victor Roadster in some markets), with Grand Prix and Enduro racing versions (GP and E) now homologated and on sale. The first batch of engines had sandcast cases built to Grand Prix specification, plus four built to Enduro specification.

By early 1966 the first batch of engines had been used up, with the last frames from the first run built up into GP versions using engines taken from the B44: volume B44E production was underway by January 1966 so engines were no longer sandcast. However, not all the works engines had magnesium alloy cases: there were also sandcast aluminium alloy cases – including the early production GPs – capable of taking the 441 or 494cc barrel – with a broader crankcase opening. From here the GP continued in limited production to January 1968, following the end of B44E production the previous March. The stud spacings increased from 74mm for the 441, 78mm for the works 494, and ultimately 80mm for the B50.

Inevitably BSA decided to cash in on Jeff Smith's success and popularity by putting versions of his bike up for sale. First was the 79 x 90mm bore and stroke, 441cc, 1965 competition-only B44GP Victor Grand Prix Scrambler, complete with an oil-in-frame made of Reynolds tubing, as on Smith's bike. It was quickly followed by the more sedate B44VE Victor Enduro, or simply the 441 Victor in the US. Sensing more appetite for the big single, in 1967 BSA offered a road-going

1971 BSA B50 racer. The beautiful polished aluminium bodywork is a change from modern plastic. Owned by Tom Ewing. STEVE KING

Phil Davis won a prize for his 1968 BSA B44 Shooting Star restoration. CRAIG HOWELL

version, the B44VR Victor Roadster, sold from 1968 in the US as the B44SS Shooting Star.

Despite big singles now being something of an oddity in a world of parallel twins, the 30bhp BSA was greeted with enthusiasm. *Cycle* magazine wrote that it was 'one of the best motorcycles made by anybody, for anything' – and this after berating the BSA's regular refusal to start, blaming the 'singularly evil' Amal carburettor. But once running, the Victor Roadster/Shooting Star impressed with its snickerty perfect gear change, lack of vibration(!) and easy acceleration right up to a modest maximum of 95mph (153km/h). The 8in front and 7in rear drums were no better nor worse than other bikes.

Yet there was little question that this was a model with a limited future. Its reason for being was off-road competition, and in knobbly tyre trim the Victor was under siege from the two-strokes. On road tyres it competed with twins, now joined by triples and fours. The final year for the 441cc single was 1970, enlarged for 1971 by increasing the bore to 84mm to create the 34bhp 499cc B50.

All the B50s had an oil-in-frame chassis (the roadster B44s had a separate oil tank) and stronger crankcases, cylinder head and cylinder. In an innovative design the electrics lived in a single removable pod, but otherwise production costs were kept down by using parts across a range of models, launched in 1971. About 5,700 were built, including some modified by specialist off-road builders such as Eric Cheney.

There were three models: the B50SS Gold Star 'street scrambler' for road use and targeting the US market; the B50T aimed at the booming trail-riding sector, again in the US, a hybrid of the SS and MX models; and the B50MX, specifically for off-road competition. The final MXs were badged as the Triumph TR5MX, the Triumph name surviving BSA's collapse.

B50s enjoyed some surprising racing successes on tarmac. A modestly upgraded B50 Gold Star 500 entered by Mead and Tomkinson and ridden by Nigel Rollason and Clive Brown won the 500cc class in both the Thruxton 500-miler and the Barcelona 24 Horas, and the Zolder 24-hour race outright. Mead and Tomkinson's B50 also held the class lap record in the Isle of Man's Production TT.

But in truth the Triumph twin was better suited to road racing than the B50, and once again underlines the rivalry rather than co-operation between the factories, which would come to a head with the 750cc triple.

AN UPGRADED 250

Where the original C15 had to compete against fairly ordinary British competition or little known oriental names, the world had moved on when BSA relaunched the C15 as first the rather staid Sportsman, and then the altogether flashier C25 Barracuda and B25 Starfire. Using the Victor bottom end, and ball and roller main bearings, allowed BSA to rejoin the chase for power without expecting the big end to fail. First up was the (claimed) 85mph (137km/h) Sportsman for 1966, often called the SS80 – but, *Motor Cycle*'s Bob Currie noted, 'The 1966 version isn't quite the SS80 we've known these past five years.'

Motor Cycling's Bernal Osborne reported on the Sportsman in the era's typically equivocal style:

> *Same engine [with the Victor bottom end], high-compression piston, sports cams, bigger-than-C15 inlet valve and carburettor, yes, but close-ratio gears are no longer fitted. Instead, the box houses the standard C15 cogs. The final-drive sprocket is one tooth smaller than standard to give lower ratios all round.*

Externally, too, there were a couple of innovations. In place of the previous nacelle, there was now a separate chromed

B25SS Victor, BSA taking a glorious name in the hope of selling a few more 250s. It was also badged Street Scrambler. STEVE GLOVER

A late C15SS with a much commented-upon humped seat. CHRISPIXONE

A 1967 C25 Barracuda, seemingly much enjoyed. GENI

headlamp, and the seat was what Bob called 'a fashionable humpy-rump pattern'. As before, the model had rich blue paint with chromed mudguards and tank panels. Bob implored:

> *Don't dismiss the sporty seat as a gimmick, for it has a whole lot in its favour. For one thing, it has much softer upholstery than the earlier one, and the one-piece covering has no seam around the upper edge to chafe the inside of the thighs. As a result, the Sportsman is a more comfortable model on which to cover longish journeys – and cover long journeys the test mount certainly did, being used for Scottish Six Days Trial reportage, various Birmingham to London trips, and general scudding around at weekends.*

Still concerned we might not like the seat, Bob promised that: 'The rear hump might have looked a bit café racer-

1969 Starfire. SG2012

like, but it did have the practical merit of keeping the pillion passenger securely anchored during rapid getaways.' Either that seat had to go – or the C15 needed restyling to suit something so *avant-garde*.

Cue the C25 Barracuda, with a new, square-finned barrel that hid the pushrod tubes (overhead valves now being seriously old fashioned), and an all-new crankshaft assembly featuring a one-piece forging with shell bearings and an alloy conrod. BSA confidently raised compression and a too-hot-to-touch cam: they stepped away from such radicalism for the following year's B25 Starfire, but compression was back up to 10:1 for 1969. Along with a 28mm Amal, this gave a claimed 25bhp and 85mph (137km/h), genuinely competitive if astounding, given the C15 origins.

Styling was also several leagues ahead of the C15. A sharply styled fibreglass tank and side panels in contemporary colours with a loud-and-proud BSA badge were right on target for the sixteen-year-old hell bent on speed and damn the fuel consumption – and reliability. Unfortunately these aspects made it less appealing in Fleetstar guise, suitably detuned and with C15 looks to woo police and other fleet buyers.

1970 brought an even more stylish street scrambler, the B25SS, and the B25ST trial version with the usual high mudguard and knobbly tyres makeover. Both were also sold as Triumphs – but the end was nigh. If you could accept the reliability issues, these were good bikes, but the competition was fierce. Those pesky Honda twins now represented the sensible shoes option up against the two-stroke twins from Suzuki and Yamaha, never mind the Kawasaki triple. And if your heart was set on a four-stroke single, Ducati offered the sublime overhead-cam Mark 3 and the even sportier Desmo.

The 250 market had become ever more important, because, increasingly riders stepped from a 250 into a car rather than on to a bigger bike. From 1971 sixteen-year-olds were limited to 'mopeds' (50cc motorcycles with pedals), with a motorcycle of up to 250cc only permitted to those with a provisional licence once they turned seventeen. This meant that a motorcycle was now in direct competition with a car, and parents (who were often signatories to finance agreements) tended to support the latter. Many would still buy a 250 as a means of transport until the car test was passed, but their number was dwindling, and a 250 needed to be something special to persuade a teenager to stick with two wheels. You would surely have to be a huge BSA aficionado to choose a B25 and, increasingly, nobody did. Thus BSA was losing the battle to get people to join their fan base and move on to a big twin, which was a shame, because even if the C15 had been slightly underwhelming, that was never true of the big twins.

CHAPTER ELEVEN

PART OF THE UNION II: MODERNIZING THE TWINS

In 1962 BSA announced that their big twins would join the singles in becoming unit construction. The reasons were the same as for the singles: a more oil-tight, stronger motor that vibrated less. For the more powerful twins it also allowed a wider, triplex primary chain, something not fitted to pre-unit motors because it risked an owner not perfectly aligning the gearbox following chain adjustment. This could damage the crank or the gearbox, or most likely both.

The big downside of BSA's unit-construction design was the so-called 'power egg' styling that gave the engine a unified, fully enclosed look, on the right especially, that was fashionable at the time. This was the age of headlamp nacelles, Ariel Arrows and Triumph bathtubs being forced on to an unconvinced public, with even Vincent getting in on the act with the Black Knight. On the filthy winter roads of Britain anything that made cleaning a motorcycle easier had

A BSA big twin for all tastes. In the foreground is a Firebird Scrambler.

1969 A50 Royal Star, the US 500 model. MF HUTCHINS

some merit, but the Americans would have none of it, paying to have a twin carburettor head fitted to the stripped-down, sportier TR6 rather than buy Edward Turner's Triumph range-topping 'streamliners'. Even the first Bonneville, with its deep mudguards, headlamp nacelle and bathtub, was held back by the US importers until something they felt was more saleable arrived from Triumph.

Eventually the designers got the message, and the fashion for full enclosure passed, as all fads do. Headlight nacelles disappeared (briefly resurfacing on the Honda CX500) – and after all, changing them for a traditional headlamp shell was easy and inexpensive. But BSA's rotund crankcases remained until the end as they were far too costly to change, and a lumpen reminder to Triumph, busy on their own unit-construction 500 and 650s for 1963, not to repeat the mistake.

More successful was BSA's one-piece finned rocker cover that was almost Art Deco graceful, with the wonderful advantage of making tappet adjustment just about a pleasure. Triumph owners, meanwhile, had to fiddle with four separate covers and far less access once they were removed.

Inside the BSA it was the curate's as well as power egg: good in parts. The part that became notorious was the timing side crankshaft bush through which oil passed on its way to the big ends. Wear here, or a drop in oil pressure, led to the far (left-hand) big end failing. This is more likely to be an issue decades later, because the oil pump was cast from an alloy that would flow into complex moulds without leaving voids, but an alloy that could warp and, with age, start to flake or crumble. The final BSA twin, the A70, had a cast-iron pump to address the issue, but that took until 1970 and a need to homologate a 750 to race in the US. Once again, this was just the nature of the industry: like all 'new' British motorcycles, BSA's A50 and A65 had their failings, but these would be gradually resolved over time in an evolutionary rather than revolutionary way. How could BSA know if a new model would be reliable? Their customers told them.

The earlier non-unit twins have a large primary chain cover that makes them look like unit construction on the drive/left side. This is an A7 Shooting Star.

An A10, again a pre-unit BSA twin. The easiest way to tell them from the unit-construction models (apart from looking at the right-hand side!) is the rocker covers: domed on the pre-unit, finned on the unit motors.

A friend embarks on a rebuild of his A65, circa 1979.

Occasionally even this piecemeal approach went wrong, spectacularly so in 1966 when BSA changed the caged ball main bearing to a roller race. This removed the positive location of the crankshaft, and could allow play, damaging the shims and thrust washer supposed to prevent lateral movement. Ultimately the timing side main bush shifted, cutting off the oil supply to the crankshaft completely, with disastrous results. Not surprisingly today's aftermarket industry can solve the problem completely, something that the BSA factory never seemed to manage.

And yet they had plenty of experience with the design, little changed in essence from the original A10 and its A7 sibling. Although there were very few parts carried over from the previous BSA twins (unlike Triumph who carried over the crank, cams and top end from pre-unit to unit), the basic internal architecture of the A50/65 motor changed little in the transition to unit construction. There remained a 360-degree one-piece crank with alloy conrods, a single cam (rather than Triumph's two) behind the cylinder block driven by a gear train on the right side, and the primary chain and clutch on the left with the same basic gearbox. All of this was assembled in new vertically split engine cases, the primary chain in the left half, the gearbox housing in the right.

Most parts and dimensions were common, including the 74mm stroke. The A50's 65.5mm bore gave 499cc, the A65's 75mm 654cc, almost square and giving the motor a revvier nature than Triumph's long stroke 71 x 82mm 650. The gear change became 'up for up'. Although still partially brazed lug, the new frame echoed the outgoing A7 and A10, although more heavily braced around the steering-head swinging-arm pivot. 'Silentbloc' swinging-arm bushes were rubber bonded to inner and outer steel sleeves, and a devil to replace once they perished. With a hydraulic damped fork and twin rear Girling dampers, the full double cradle chassis could, in its day, justly claim to be the best handling package available that wasn't a Norton Featherbed.

Both the A50 and A65 were launched with alloy heads and single carburettor, offering 28.5bhp at 6,000rpm and 38bhp at 5,800rpm respectively. Indeed, aside from the engine top end and minor cosmetic differences, the only parts that weren't shared between the two new models were the single leading shoe front brake, 8in on the bigger bike and an inch less on the A50. Perhaps oddly, they were catalogued as the Star in Britain, and the Royal Star in the US – a country that had famously waged war to be free of the monarchy. Perhaps that is why the new models didn't sell as well as had been hoped – but more likely, it was the frankly dowdy styling.

To set off the rotund power-egg motor BSA had screwed on perhaps the largest side panels ever fitted to a motorcycle, big pressed steel covers that offered smooth lines and covered all those bits and pieces – including the dry sump motor's oil tank – that get packaged below a rider's seat. Presumably due to costs, these would survive almost until the end, only replaced by more modest and stylish fittings when the oil-in-frame chassis arrived for 1971.

ALL COME TO LOOK FOR AMERICA

By 1959 UK motorcycle demand had peaked, but the US, and the west coast especially, was still booming. Reading the history it almost feels as if BSA decided that they would serve the sensible Brits, while Triumph would go after the decadent Americans. JoMo, Triumph's eastern distributor, also brought in Daimler for a while, and Ariel until they realized a Red Hunter was never going to find a buyer when there was a Triumph twin in the showroom. Little wonder BSA put Ariel out of their misery in 1967, only to revive it for ritual humiliation with the Ariel 3.

Despite this, however, BSA actually had more dealerships than Triumph in the US until the late fifties. Even by 1959 BSA had 250 outlets to JoMo's 150, and almost 100 more BSAs than Triumphs were sold in the States that year. But Bill Johnson was very aware that his private enterprise must be in BSA's sights, with the wholly owned subsidiary TriCo also outperforming his dealers and a Triumph franchise often openly referred to as a licence to print money within the trade. Indeed, even Harley-Davidson had taken umbrage at British success in conquering their home turf, and complained to the tariffs commission in 1952 that, rather than growing the market, BSA and Triumph were stealing sales that were Harley's by rights. Partisan US magazines had supported Harley by playing down how well the Brits were doing, although eventually would reflect what was of interest to their readers and advertising department.

However, Harley's complaint ended in farce when, after British motorcycles had been brought into the tariffs commission, proceedings were halted while Harley had to disassemble their big V-twins to get them into the lift. The committee eventually reported that Harley's market sector was completely different to the segment that BSA and Triumph were creating. Shortly afterwards Harley announced its own 750.

But the number of BSA versus Triumph sales from the mid to late fifties didn't tell the whole story: a lot of BSA sales were Gold Stars, and these would look dated with the arrival of the unit singles. Perhaps more importantly, BSA

A later A65 Lightning, with a restyled fuel tank. RONALD SAUNDERS

The first Lightnings had this distinctive gold paintwork. Note the twin carburettors.

had, as legendary racer Stan Dibben averred a few chapters ago, no interest in US fashions such as high handlebars and fringed leather saddles, jackets and saddlebags. The photographs of the era look high camp today to anyone brought up with motorcycling in the UK: the first time that most of us saw leather peaked caps and fringed leather chaps was on a character in *The Village People*. By the time 1953's *Wild One* was granted an audience in the UK in 1967 – with an X certificate – motorcycling and society had changed beyond recognition.

At Triumph, however, Edward Turner had fallen head over heels in love with America, especially southern California. He spent six months a year Stateside, never looking happier than when photographed in Columbia Studio's sound lot aboard a Triumph twin with Rita Hayworth on the pillion. And no moody black leather for Turner: he was wearing a double-breasted blazer, two-tone shoes and a big grin. Turner saw the Californians love of chrome, high exhausts, higher handlebars and bright colours at first hand. He saw the stripped-back 'desert sleds', he saw the joy of riding in sunshine. BSA, on the other hand, saw that they were outselling Triumph, and thought no more about the future. The road tests admitted that the BSA twins handled better than the Triumphs and were often faster, and the Americans seemed happy with the A50 and A65 as long as it had high handlebars and the smaller export fuel tank.

It was 1964 before BSA seemed to realize they had to act. The new unit-construction Triumph twins were far outselling the BSA equivalents, which couldn't even match the glories of the old A7 and A10. US tuners were learning how to make the Triumph twins the fastest motorcycles in racing, and the US distributors were learning how to make everybody want a Triumph so successfully that Honda would simply copy everything they did – apart from building motors that leaked oil. Everybody knew that big twins leaked oil, whether they came from Britain or the US. And then Honda launched the CB450, and people, especially on the American west coast, realized it didn't have to be this way.

It was in quality control, as much as, if not more than, in new models, that BSA failed to invest. They were no better or worse than their fellow British manufacturers, which probably exacerbated their complacency. But across the Atlantic, Americans no longer accepted it was normal for motors to leak oil, for components to break and for Joe Lucas to completely misunderstand electricity. Used to big, unstressed motors in cars and motorcycles that had to cover big distances, Americans demanded reliability. The importers begged BSA, and Turner especially, to introduce new quality control measures both in house and with suppliers to make sure things worked before they were put into production. They also wanted to be shipped models that dealers could sell, rather than makeweights. BSA listened politely, looked at the costs involved, and did nothing. Pat Slinn thinks it wouldn't even have been difficult or expensive to address:

> *For the works bikes, even the press bikes, we used Allen screws and made sure the mating surfaces were flat. An A65 was a superb bike that just shouldn't leak oil if it's put it together properly. But you went on to the production line, and people were just chucking castings about, which didn't help. With Allen screws and a bit of care there'd have been no oil leaks. The bikes could have been so much better with a little care… and BSA was running some wonderful ads in the US that must have been getting them plenty of attention.*

BSA had indeed noticed that Triumph in the US was running glamorous advertisements promising irresistible attraction to the opposite sex in the pages of magazine road tests and in competition. So the Star range exploded – occasionally literally – for 1964. As well as the basic A50 and A65, and fundamentally identical police versions, there was a plethora of performance options. Two new 500 models were introduced in the States, both with twin carburettors, designated the Cyclone Road and the Cyclone Competition. The former was fitted with a sports cam, and the competition version was supplied without lights and with a higher compression ratio and race cam. Both had the 8in SLS front brake from the 650. There were also a handful – perhaps twenty – Wasps, another 500cc off-road competitor, and a little brother to the brace of 650 BSA Hornets offered during 1966 and 1967.

The 'big tank' Mark III Spitfire, again with twin carburettors.

US market Spitfires gained restyled fuel tanks, always smaller than the UK models and with higher handlebars. Note the pre-unit twin to the right.

SPORTING CHOICES

The sporting 650 rider was now spoilt for choice. Camshaft profiles, compression ratios and carburettor speciation climbed as the power rose: in order of performance came the A65R Rocket, the A65T Thunderbolt Rocket, A65L Lightning Rocket, and finally the stripped down 'desert sled' that was the A65SH Spitfire Hornet. There were handsome high-level silencers, Siamesed exhausts and well-advertised 'speed victories': wins at the 1963 150-mile road race; the 1964 Ascot Speedway 8-mile National; the 1965 24-hour Marathon and the 50-mile National. In advertising the latter, BSA proclaimed the Lightning 'America's favourite super sports 650'.

But actor Steve McQueen tested the BSA Hornet, and came away less than impressed: 'A keen bike – but I found it awfully heavy', and he suggested that a less steep steering-head angle would offer 'a more stable ride in the rough'. McQueen would buy his first Husqvarna, a 360cc two-stroke, in 1968, suggesting it wasn't the BSA, it was just that the strokers were taking over in true dirt racing. This also underlined a difference between the US west and east coast markets: California was a land of sunshine and sand, the east rather more like Europe. A four-stroke big twin might be fun in the former, but it was going to be thrashed in competition in the latter.

The 500cc BSA twins met with limited success in AMA (American Motorcyclist Association, the equivalent to Britain's ACU) road racing and, off road, riders still stuck with their single-cylinder 500cc Gold Stars. Anyway, as Triumph could have told them, in the United States the 650 was the big seller. There were now 12-volt Lucas alternators and a hotter coil ignition and brighter lights. There was also a switch to the new Smith's magnetic units, rather than the older chronometric (mechanical) instruments.

You don't have to be a management consultant or production engineer to realize that BSA had gone from a pared-back range of motorcycles aimed at everyday riders to a performance-fixated brand determined to give Triumph a bloody nose in the US. But while this was being fought out in development workshops, racetracks and showrooms, seismic changers were afoot in BSA's management.

In 1962 Doug Hele rejoined the BSA group from Norton, persuaded by fellow defector Bert Hopwood, to take command of Triumph's experimental department. More controversially, BSA brought in consultants McKinsey and Company on board to streamline BSA and Triumph's operations and product. There were no ashen faces when it suggested

The Firebird Scrambler was another of BSA's successful 'street scrambler' models so popular in the US. The high-level exhaust could be factory fitted.

Another later model Lightning, again in US specification. The lack of silencers is not a factory option, other than for the competition versions, which also lacked lighting.

'integration' of the factories' operations, including in the US where there was a growing realization that the Japanese were dominating the market.

Eric Turner, now group chairman having been at BSA since 1960, decided that McKinsey's sales projections weren't high enough, believing BSA and Triumph could steal Japan's market share given that they had no big bikes to sell. And yet BSA had no market-leading lightweights, which were exactly what the Japanese and Italians were selling. But Turner (no relation to Edward) ignored dealers' and distributors' advice, and instead had his accountants make sales projections. Honda, meanwhile, while treating its dealers like royalty, by 1963 was selling more bikes in the US than the rest of the motorcycle industry put together.

In other news Bridgestone started making motorcycles, two-stroke 90 and 175cc motorcycles, but would be persuaded by the other Japanese factories to focus on tyres, leaving the Big Four – Honda, Yamaha, Suzuki and Kawasaki – to plan world domination. More happily for the British, the FIM granted motocross racing world championship status, which BSA would twice win. You can see why, to the British motorcycle industry, the glass looked half full, rather than half empty.

But should it have looked that way? BSA closed the Ariel factory at Selly Oak, the final Leader and Arrows being built at BSA's factory in Small Heath. The previous year Edward Turner, apparently bitter at the direction the company was taking, retired as head of the Automotive Division (which still included motorcycles), although he hung on to his BSA directorship. Bert Hopwood had hoped to be Turner's successor, but the job went to BSA's Harry Sturgeon, who was determined to merge BSA and Triumph. He was liked and his decisions respected, but a brain tumour ended his career and ultimately his life. His replacement in 1966 would be an altogether different character, for whom much criticism has been reserved: Lionel Jofef, brought in from the aircraft industry and in many eyes the architect of BSA's demise.

But perhaps the end was already in sight. The arrival of the Honda CB450 'Black Bomber' might have left the British press nonplussed – they had expected something more exotic and closer to Honda's grand prix racers, although the road-going fours would arrive soon enough. In the meantime the ACU viewed the CB450 exotic enough to bar Mike Hailwood from racing one at the 1966 Brands Hatch 500-mile race, taking exception to the double overhead cams and torsion-bar valve springs. Even now the decision is controversial and hints at protectionism – but once the CB750 had arrived, the ACU relented and the Bomber would go on to win the 1969 and 1971 Production TT titles with a Suzuki T500 splitting the Hondas in 1970.

If the CB450's sales were only so-so in Blighty, over in the US the bike rapidly became a favourite, especially after a restyle from the rather staid launch model. Just a year or so into its life-cycle the bike received a fifth gear, a disc brake and year-on-year cosmetic changes, the CB450 remaining on the books until 1974. That might seem like a lifetime, but even by 1974, the British thought of electric starts, five-speed gearboxes and disc brakes as superfluous foreign luxuries, even if motorcycle disc brakes were pioneered by an Englishman, Colin Lyster, whose ideas were endorsed by Mike Hailwood. Lyster had tried to sell his disc-brake patents to BSA, who rejected them. In the end AP Lockheed bought the rights in 1967, BSA instead setting about developing new conical drum brakes.

But even the conical brakes were not a priority and, for 1966, BSA's 650 twins just got new forks and a modified rear brake. As money got tight, rationalization finally took grip. The A50 was largely left to its own devices, management at last grasping that the public were in thrall to BSA's rather magnificent big singles, with the halo effect of Jeff Smith's world championship still writ large in the firmament. The 650 was now only available as the Thunderbolt or Lightning, the former with a single carburettor and 41bhp, the latter with twin Amals and 53bhp.

Variations on a theme followed, including the Lightning Clubman, Spitfire Hornet and Firebird. The Firebird was a street scrambler, a category BSA could claim to have invented with the 1964 Hornet. Originally a competition model, US dealers soon discovered that buyers craved the look and would forego the hairy racing tweaks for a state of tune that made the bike easier to ride in exchange for a lighting kit that turned the BSA into a big pussycat with the look of a tiger (without the Triumph model's capital T).

This rationalization also involved the BSA group buying up JoMo, consolidating it with TriCor, alongside Hap Alzima's BSA distribution in the US. In theory, bringing all the administration, distribution and marketing of Triumph and BSA under one stateside roof saved a fortune, made production planning a doddle, and carried no downsides at all. Except when dealers of both brands were told to offer both Triumph and BSA models they viewed it as it the 'merger from Hell'. Many quit in protest, and Pat Slinn understands why:

A late model, c. 1970, Firebird Scrambler. The exhaust system, including the heat shield, was standard.

'The competition between Triumph and BSA in the UK was fierce, especially between racing departments, but it was good-natured. In America they hated each other, they really did.'

For example, Doug Hele had developed the 500cc Tiger 100 into a racer, winning the 1966 American Daytona 200 race, repeating the win in 1967. BSA management should have been pleased, especially as the resulting new model, the twin carburettor Daytona 500, was another immediate hit. But no, BSA set out to beat Triumph at their own game. Pat Slinn again:

> *BSA built six A50 500 twin-cylinder road racers for Daytona in 1967. They recruited Alan Shepherd, who rode a Matchless to second place (behind Hailwood) in the 1962 and 1963 500cc world championship to oversee the project.*
>
> *Alan had been one of the very best privateers and an MZ works rider. He had been offered a Honda contract in about 1964/5 and had crashed a Honda six (I think) at Suzuka in Japan whilst testing. He was seriously injured, and he had also banged his head. He made a long recovery, but never raced again. When*

I first met him at BSA he seemed a nice guy; however, he did have a strange personality, which was put down to his accident in Japan. Not many people liked him, and many couldn't get on with him, especially Clive Bennett (ex-Ariel), and Clive suggested that he shouldn't go to Daytona.

Alan did a good job supervising the build of the bikes, but not the engines! The evening before the bikes were due to be crated up and sent to the US, Alan took out the last one to be finished on to the BSA test track just to make sure that they worked. Unfortunately he hadn't realized that it was after 4:30pm and the factory would turn out at 5pm. The exit from the factory workers' car parks led on to part of the test track and a red/white barrier was lowered to stop traffic passing. Alan didn't notice this barrier and crashed straight into it; he was badly hurt and was taken off to the hospital. The bike was quite badly damaged and we worked most of the evening, night and morning rebuilding it.

The bikes didn't do very well in the Daytona 200; I think they all packed up! They were fitted with a Joe Hunt ignition system at the request of the BSA importers – I believe that was OK on the short track bikes, but not on the road racers. Also the engines suffered with silly mechanical problems during practice because they hadn't had enough development time before they were sent to the US. There was a big, not very pleasant debriefing and investigation back at Small Heath. Clive Bennett was the development engineer in charge of this project, and as such took most of the blame. His reputation was damaged after this.

I met Alan again at a dealer exhibition in about 1987 – he remembered me and we spoke a lot; he was very bitter about the way he had been treated by some of the BSA people. Alan also said that the Daytona 200 A50 engines had not had enough development time either on the dynamometer or in track testing. I felt that I should apologize to him about what he told me how he was treated. He died a few years ago.

Triumph finished first and second in the 1967 Daytona 200, and that really did rile some of the BSA people. In all honesty BSA should have taken it more seriously and started earlier with the building and development of the A50s, and thrown more resources at the job. Some powerful people in BSA disliked road racing, and didn't like anything that took money and resources form the trials and scrambles bikes. Triumph had a dedicated road race department and sent their own engineers and mechanics to look after their bikes: BSA East and West Coast relied on their own mechanics and BSA Small Heath sent one person, Clive Bennett, and a publicity guy! Needless to say the 'publicity guy' had little to do.

Meanwhile the evolution of the 650 twins had slowed to glacial. Demand from the US meant that the factory was working at beyond capacity, with serious consequences for quality. For 1968 there were Amal concentric rather than Monobloc carburettors, and the Lightning got an 8in twin leading shoe (TLS) front brake that was copied on to the Thunderbolt for 1969. There were new badges and colours and for 1970, a new(ish) fuel tank and exhaust balance pipes: these were in response to tightening noise restrictions in Germany and the US especially.

By 1967 the US market had reached what the marketing people called 'maturity' – not a phrase often associated with motorcycling. But, as with the UK in 1959, what was meant was that purchases were largely replacements and bought by enthusiasts. In the US in 1967 only 30 per cent of sales were

Oil-in-frame Lightning Scrambler. The grey paint on the frame was supposed to hint at the titanium of the factory motocrossers, but was unpopular for showing dirt – and oil.

Pat Slinn testing an oil-in-frame twin.
COLLECTION OF PAT SLINN

to those joining the sport – good news for BSA, who had little to offer a beginner but plenty for the committed fan looking to trade up. BSA's other interests and research and development may have been costing a fortune, but modest tweaks on the existing range were all that was needed to keep the factories at full tilt. Indeed, this was causing serious problems.

Not only was there a knock-on effect on (a lack of) quality control, there were faults from bought-in equipment. Faulty ignition on 1966 650s led to overheating and seizures and, separately, there were incidents of pistons and valves colliding. By this time Pat Slinn was working with BSA in Germany, confronted by the enthusiasm of US servicemen. 'They would bring bikes in, looking at the floor, saying "it just stopped running". Of course they'd been drag racing them, running them up to 10,000rpm or something, then wondering why they stopped. The 650s were strong bikes, but they were never built to put up with that.'

Those that were shipped off to the US were packed so closely that subframes would buckle and seats refuse to fit. One shipment of 4,000 bikes to the US was so badly damaged by salt on their Atlantic crossing that the Americans just sent them straight back to Small Heath.

The pressure to get the bikes built and shipped out led to BSA winning a Queen's Award to Industry for Export Achievement in 1967 and 1968, and great praise from government and the business community. After cars and Scotch whiskey, motorcycles were the UK's biggest export in an age of economic turmoil, a horrific balance of payments deficit, and sterling's devaluation. But this much-vaunted success came at a hefty cost, as Pat Slinn remembers:

> *I was asked into a meeting with the American importers, and they just sat on one side of the table lining up small bits of blue plastic. Eventually I realized they were bits of biro caps: it turned out that they were being used as a quick check on the production line that oil levels were where they should be. Every now and then a cap would fall off, but nobody said anything. Sooner or later they broke up in the gearbox or something.*
>
> *Another time there weren't enough gudgeon pins to complete a build, so steel rod was used instead, and the Americans were warned not to start the engines and that they'd get replacement gudgeon pins as soon as possible. There was a joke that every A65 went out with the tank stuffed with cash for the warranty claims.*

Indeed. During the late sixties the US dealers reckoned they were claiming an average of $800 for every BSA 650 they sold – about half of the list price, and more than the dealer would make on the sale. In the face of this – bearing in mind that such issues could lead to a buyer demanding his cash back or miss a season's riding – BSA's largely cosmetic updates of the big twins sounds like deckchairs being unstacked on the *Titanic* in the hope of catching the following day's sunshine. And it sort of was. The rumour of the CB750 was floated in one of Harry Sturgeon's first board meetings as chairman in 1964. Understandably there was sheer panic, even though at this stage nobody knew that it would have 4 cylinders.

It was this that led to the explosive upgrading of the 650 range and, more importantly, Hopwood and Hele's 'Speed Twin-and a half' being green lighted. *Motor Cycle*'s Vic Willoughby had signed off his 1967 interview with Hele observing that '...a high-performance seven-fifty parallel twin is not exactly at the top of the desirability stakes.' Hele knew that the Trident/Rocket III was already ready for production, but that's for the next chapter. In fact BSA needed 'a high-performance seven-fifty parallel twin' even after the triple made it into production.

THE END OF THE LINE

Hele might not have believed a 750 twin was an answer, but he was, as far as American racers were concerned, asking the wrong question. Dick Mann especially wanted one, and with a BSA 751cc A70 would win his final – of twenty-four – AMA Nationals in August 1972 at Peoria in Illinois.

BSA had wanted to squeeze 750cc from their parallel twin to compete in the open class AMA racing since 1969. The rules required that entries were based on a motorcycle that the public could buy, with a big but: Harley had shamelessly persuaded the AMA to limit ohv (that is, British) motors to 500cc while allowing Harley to run their side-valve V-twins at 750cc. And then, from 1969, the AMA allowed 750cc bikes of all types to enter, as long as at least 200 examples of the model had been built. Harley quickly converted its side-valve 'flathead' KRs into the ohv Sportster-based XR750, with great success. Triumph and BSA now had their 750 triples, Honda their new four, and Triumph bumped their 650 Bonneville up to 750cc (in a rather underhand way, converting the bikes in the US), all eligible for Grand National flat track races. But racers wanted the traction of a twin if they were to win, and buyers wanted whatever the racers could win with.

The 1971 A70 Lightning was BSA's answer, 202 being built between June and August 1971. Around 180 were shipped to BSA's East Coast distributor, with the remaining twenty-two sent to the West. Only distinguishable at first glance by the side panel '750' decal, all were painted the same orange and off-white used on the 650. Most had black frames, while a few had the pale grey frames that BSA briefly used early in the season. The engine cases were externally identical to the 650's, but with a narrower timing side bush to accommodate the new crankshaft with an 85mm stroke, up from 74mm with bore remaining at 75mm. Conrods were the same length as the 650, but with steel rather than alloy caps, and fitted to gudgeon pins set lower in new pistons. Despite these having a gentler domed top than the 650's, compression was up to 9.5:1 from the 650's 9.0:1. The A70 ran two Amal 930 concentric carburettors with 250 main jets, larger than the A65. As already noted, the oil pump was cast iron rather than alloy and of a higher capacity. 52bhp at 6,250rpm (the same as the 650, but at 750 fewer rpm) and a top speed of 120mph (193km/h) was claimed.

The 751cc A70 twin, built to homologate a bigger motor for racing in the US. BONHAMS

The chassis for the entire 650 range was updated alongside the launch of the A70. Along with the Triumph twins, virtually everything was changed for 1971, with the exception of the engines. A new frame from the almost comically misguided Umberslade Hall R&D team, led by chief stylist Stephen Mettam, was the centrepiece of the revamp, an overhaul that ignored everything the customer base wanted fixed, such as oil leaks, vibration and flaky electrics. The so called 'oil-bearing frame' had the engine oil in a 3in (76mm) diameter spine, clearing out the need for an oil tank (which was increasingly prone to splitting) under the seat. New conical brakes were pretty but ineffective compared to the disc brakes people had expected.

The new bodywork brought mixed reactions: it certainly gave the 650 range a more modern look, and to the writer's eye was far more attractive than what had gone before. But it turned off traditionalists, who were BSA's core market, without offering the reliability and oil-tight smoothness of the big Japanese multis that younger buyers were lapping up.

Inevitably for a professional racer Dick Mann ran his A70 motor in a bespoke chassis, rather than the hated oil-in-frame architecture. Immediately dubbed 'too tall' by the press, the 1971 range was a belated attempt at rationalization as well as modernization, which caused endless problems – including new places for oil leaks to spring from – for both Triumph and BSA. What were they thinking of? Sighs Pat Slinn:

> *I've no idea. Maybe the race department thought it was a good idea. It had worked on Smithy's [Jeff Smith's] bike and the Victor, so maybe someone thought it would work on the twins. The reason they painted it that silly grey was to make it look like Smithy's titanium frame. Still, at least they didn't paint the silencers.*

Ah, yes – painting the silencers. Another idea from Umberslade Hall that was the black hole sucking in money and sales as it tried to make BSA motorcycles – and especially the new 750 triple – appeal to everybody except the motorcycle-buying public. Meriden was left to work out how to fit their 650 twins in the new frame, and persuaded Umberslade to modify it so that it was possible to lift cylinder heads without dropping the engine and, eventually, got the seat rails lowered. With that sorted Umberslade Hall could get back to trying to make the new triple unsaleable.

The styling department at Umberslade: Alf Judd on the left, Pat Slinn centre and Stephan Mettam. Alf was apparently serious about different-coloured exhaust pipes as well as silencers! COLLECTION OF PAT SLINN

A70L LIGHTNING

Year: 1971
Displacement: 751cc
Bore/stroke: 75 x 85mm
Compression ratio: 9.5:1
Engine type: Four-stroke overhead-valve vertical twin
Carburation: Twin 30mm Amal 930
Ignition system: Coil
Claimed power: 52bhp at 6,500rpm
Transmission: Multiplate wet clutch, four-speed unit-construction gearbox. Primary and final drive by chain
Brakes: Conical drums, 8in TLS front, 7in SLS rear
Wheels: 19in front, 18in rear
Chassis: Telescopic front forks, twin shock absorber rear swinging arm, duplex frame
Weight: 390lb/177kg
Top speed: 117mph (188km/h)

CHAPTER TWELVE

A DANCE IN TRIPLE TIME

Umberslade Hall is a Grade II* listed seventeenth-century mansion, these days residential apartments, near Tanworth-in-Arden, Warwickshire. But from 1967 BSA leased it, complete with peacocks roaming the classical gardens, to merge Triumph and BSA's various design and development departments. This supposed think-tank, roughly central to their factories at Meriden, Redditch and Small Heath, was dubbed a 'styling studio', and was run by an art school graduate. Soon nicknamed 'Slumberglade', this was where Pat Slinn's frustration with the British motorcycle industry started to escalate:

> *The contempt people had for Umberslade was proved when hairdressing kit was planted in the studio, and we had calls asking for hairdressing appointments. Many of the engineers came from outside motorcycling, and couldn't even ride. Nothing ever seemed to get finished, and I was glad to move on.*

So in 1970, Pat took his wife Elaine and growing family to Germany and became service manager for the BSA importer.

It was little wonder that the people at Umberslade Hall drove Pat, and many others, from within its revered walls. They had already persuaded the main board that a completely new look was essential for the 3-cylinder project, and most especially that Jack Wickes and his 'traditional' ideas should be kept well away. Hele had the engine bench tested, and the 1964 Bonneville lookalike prototype P1 running in 1965: engineers had developed the chassis in parallel with

Early BSA Rocket III, obviously restored but to factory specification.

The other side of the Rocket III. The reflectors suggest a US model.

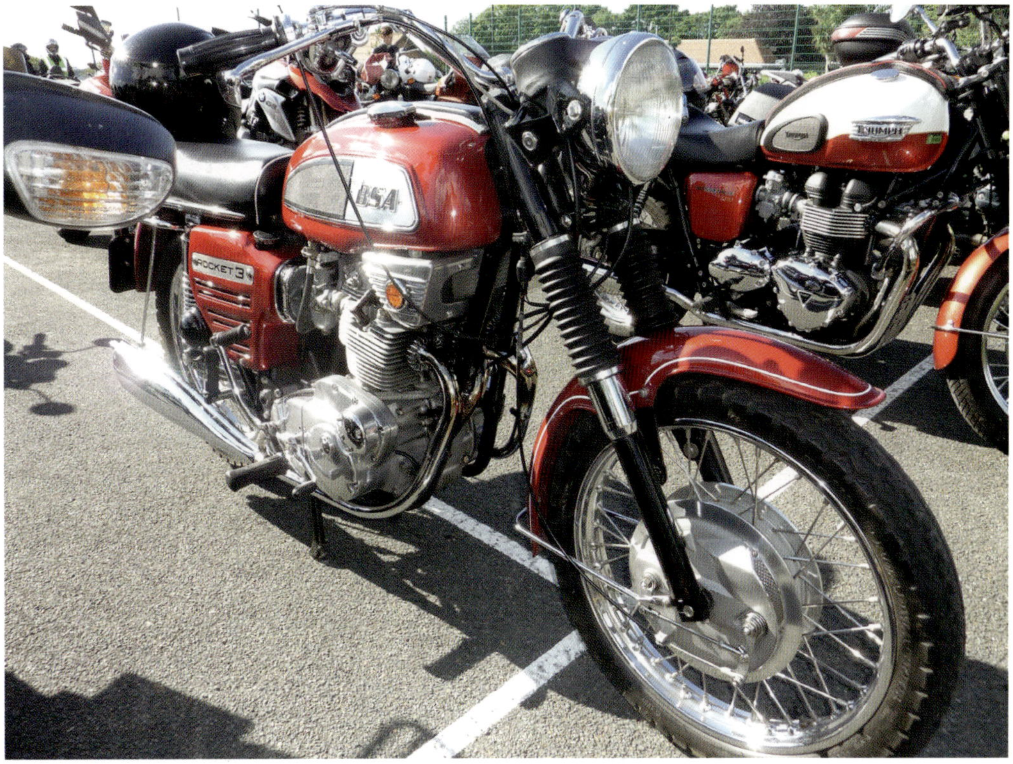

engine development by bulking up a standard 650 Bonneville with lead weights in anticipation of the triple's extra pounds.

The second prototype – 1966's P2 – erased teething problems such as overheating, wet sumping and noisy primary transmission. Production was pencilled in for 1967. It would have been a fine-looking motorcycle with world-beating performance on sale a full year before the CB750 was first shown. Instead, Ogle Design was awarded a contract to revisit the project, including styling BSA's most important motorcycle for years: the Rocket III, as BSA's literature and advertising referred to it – or Rocket 3, as the motorcycle was badged. Umberslade Hall couldn't even decide what their motorcycle was called.

Founded by David Ogle in 1954 in Letchworth – closer to London than Birmingham – Ogle Design had developed and built kit cars from 1959 on, their final car being the SX250, an updated Daimler Dart built in 1962. Two were made, but Daimler – sold in 1960 by BSA to Jaguar – weren't interested, and the design became the basis of the Reliant Scimitar GT, which appeared in 1964. Apart from this project, Ogle's most famous design before the Trident and Rocket III was the 1959 Bush TR82 portable radio. More famous work for Reliant and Raleigh – the Scimitar GTE, Bond Bug and Chopper bicycle respectively – was still a few years off and arguably only won following BSA's endorsement.

Ogle Design's work took eighteen months, and in 1967 delivered not only the infamous 'bread bin' fuel tank reminiscent of BMW's, but an extra 40lb (18kg) of weight, with the option of inclining the cylinders forwards by 15 degrees. This allowed the BSA's motor to look different to the Trident's – a ludicrously expensive way to achieve so little – but it also brought the cylinders closer to the twin down tubes of the BSA variant's A65-based frame, lowered the centre of gravity, and left room for a bigger airbox and starter motor. Little wonder that Triumph adopted the layout for the T160 Trident update. But the ridiculed 'ray gun' silencers were a worthwhile addition, despite their dubious aesthetic: they were a fine compromise between noise suppression, maximum power and production costs. And yet the motor still had just four gears, the brakes were still drums, and it was now 1968.

This was seven long years after Hopwood and Hele had first discussed the idea of a triple – smoother than a twin, narrower than a four – and four years since BSA's boss Harry Sturgeon had seen Doug Hele's completed drawings and pushed the panic button to get the triple into production before Honda's 750 arrived. And that was when many at BSA

The later Rocket III restyled for the US market. TR001

assumed the big Honda would be a twin, rather than a four.

The dream team of Hopwood and Doug Hele had been back at Triumph since 1962, and many – especially Hopwood – believed they could have pulled off a British motorcycle industry turnaround. Hopwood was working on his modular project, aiming to build a 200 single that would lead via a 350/400 twin and a 750 four to a range-topping 1000cc V5. Could it have worked? There is an example of a similar project from a decade later: in the mid-seventies Laverda raced a 1000cc V6 with the intention of a road bike and 750V4 and 350 V-twin following. Sadly raising funds for such an ambitious project in an industry seen as being on its last legs was the stumbling block.

This would be an era of inflation, high borrowing rates and currency devaluation, and it's hard to think of any such project surviving beyond an engineer's fantasy. Even the modern Norton venture is on a tiny scale compared to what Hopwood imagined achieving: Ducati probably come closest to a small-scale luxury motorcycle factory along the lines that Hopwood dreamed of, and they have only survived via some creative Italian government funding and an obstinate belief in the value of the Ducati name by people who were masters at raising money. John Bloor's Triumph venture is an exemplar and started with a less ambitious modular idea – 750cc triples and 1000cc fours – in a common chassis. But then John Bloor did it with his own money and a long-term vision, rather than cash from whimsical investors.

Hele meanwhile was working on something less ambitious but completely feasible, in essence an evolution of the Triumph 500 twin with an extra cylinder squeezed into the middle to create a 750 triple. It sounds easy, but Hele's design would be developed into the most successful race bikes of their time, evolved – that word again – from what would become the Triumph Trident and BSA Rocket III. And it was Hele's design: he was adamant that it was all his own work and that Hopwood had no claim on the project, saying later: 'He was also keen to claim credit wherever possible. The Triumph T150 triple was entirely my design, regardless of what Hopwood, or anyone else says. I drew the Triumph triple completely unaided and on my own.'

If only Hele and Wickes *had* been allowed to draw the complete motorcycle 'completely unaided'. Dealers were horrified at the Ogle makeover, the powerful and vocal American Triumph distributors especially so. They demanded – and got – what they called a 'beauty kit' to return their Tridents to something approximating the look of a Bonneville. When these failed to arrive promptly, the Americans assumed it was spite, and a device to try and get them to offload the Ogle bikes: the truth was that it was down to BSA's finances, something that the profitable Triumph subsidiary had yet to suspect.

Even so, the Rocket III/Trident was launched in September 1968, to acclamation – only to be eclipsed four weeks later by the Honda CB750 at the October 1968 Tokyo show. Compared to the British triple, the CB750 had a five-speed gearbox, overhead camshaft, oil-tight engine, electric start and a disc brake. It was also significantly cheaper than the BSA triples in America, at $1,400. The British triples, at $1,750, were about the most expensive motorcycle on the market. Not surprisingly, in 1969, the first year of production, Honda sold over 30,000 CB750s, and BSA/Triumph fewer than 7,000 triples in the US – this despite the British triple refusing to blow up – as was nearly the case.

It turned out that a curious Boston dealer had stripped the first triple delivered to him and discovered that the crankcases hadn't been flushed, and still had casting sand in them – which would have been disastrous had the motors been filled with oil and started. And this was far from the only problem – but American distributors knew the triple couldn't afford a reputation as troublesome if it was to survive Honda's onslaught. Fortunate wasn't the word for the Boston dealer's discovery.

TALKING TO THE COMPETITION

Gerald Davison was with Honda UK from 1968 to 1985, gaining influence and experience in every aspect of the business, and becoming Honda's first non-Japanese director in the process. He had a reputation for single mindedness and for making sure that Honda were top dog – at races, market share, everything – regardless of what it took. Yet if you had only ever known him in the last few decades you'd find this hard to believe of the 'old school' gentleman he now is, with a fine appreciation of antiques and a world-leading knowledge of Chinese ceramics. He had already worked at Chrysler, moving to Honda at just twenty-six, where he saw his first CB750 sent to the UK for the 1969 shows.

> *I remember the first CB750 arriving. Mr Honda understood it was about the product; he wasn't typically Japanese, he was something of a maverick with no connection to the traditional obligations, and a very flamboyant character – he liked to wear red shirts. There were perhaps fifty of us working in Power Road [Honda's UK headquarters in Chiswick, usefully close to Heathrow airport], covering all aspects of the business. I was earning my money on the car side – I'd joined on the car side – but I always got my enjoyment and excitement with the bikes. I'd trained as an assessing engineer, and every single bike that came in, came to me: within the office people said: 'Send it to Davison, he's the bike freak.' I remember helping to uncrate the first CB750: we heard this great excitement and call to rush down to the workshop. We ripped apart the crate and quickly got it running; I stood a threepenny bit [an old British coin with twelve straight sides], putting it so it stood edge on, on the tank, and we stood there mesmerized with the smoothness of the thing: I think it was a gold one for the show.*

Pat Slinn was also at that Earls Court show, part of the BSA team showing off the Rocket III:

> *I remember seeing the new Honda at the show, up on its stand, and then looking at our triples leaking oil on to the carpet. And these were our show bikes! But the biggest sin was that you couldn't buy them – there'd be rows of unfinished bikes at the factory, just waiting for something silly: probably a footrest forging or a pawl for the gearbox, but it meant they couldn't go out to the dealers.*

The Rocket III built for classic racing, giving a fine view of the motor. The retention of the standard exhaust system illustrates how good it was, despite the 'ray gun' looks.

Or to the Triumph factory at Meriden: all the 3-cylinder motors were built at Small Heath, but those looking for a Trident to call home were built by BSA at Small Heath and then trucked over to the Triumph factory. Yet instead of spending money making sure the bikes were properly screwed together and dispatched in perfect condition to eager customers, BSA management decided they needed to embark on the most expensive racing programme in the company's history. Honda had already won the 1969 Bol D'Or 24-hour race with the CB750, and was the bookies' favourite to win the Daytona 200 in February 1970. Whatever fans of the Isle of Man TT might think, by 1970 this was the most important motorcycle race on earth, held in front of the most important motorcycle market on earth.

The meeting opened the AMA road-racing season, running at a banked racetrack close to the Florida beaches that had hosted racing since 1937, and seen the construction of the International Speedway circuit in 1961. Even early in the year Florida is bathed in sunshine, and the race was a magnet for American motorcyclists. It was here that BSA decided they would give Honda a bloody nose, racing in the new Formula 750 class, which coincided nicely with the rules for AMA Grand National road races, including the prestigious Daytona 200 classic that opened the season.

The British imagined they would be more than ready for the race, despite having just six months to prepare. Mike Hailwood was paid an undisclosed amount – so much that BSA daren't admit to it – to race a Rocket III, one of six specially commissioned triples (two BSAs, four Triumphs) in Rob North frames. Three Daytona regulars and US headline stars were secured to race alongside Hailwood: Dave Aldana, Gary Nixon and Gene Romero. Just announcing the team was a huge marketing coup.

The factory concentrated on race-prepping motors, and farmed out the construction of purpose-built road-racing frames to specialist fabricator Rob North. His brazed steel-tube frames were innovative, a perimeter-style design before that term was probably coined, with top rails that ran directly from steering head to swing-arm pivot. A total of six factory machines were shipped to Daytona, three BSAs and three Triumphs, popularly called 'Beezumphs'. Despite an engine that could trace its roots all the way back to 1938, the factory triples showed speed. Decades of tuning tricks learned on Triumph twins applied equally well to the new engine – and Umberslade Hall's bodywork refined in Harrier 'Jump Jet' builder Hawker Siddeley's wind tunnel contributed to a 165mph (265km/h) top speed.

The triples went well in practice for Daytona, with Nixon claiming pole and remembering that 'the bike had radically changed the character of the previous year's race. So much power... handling and stability. The Fontana drum brakes were really the best I've ever tried. So much so that I wanted to use it the following season, while my teammates had the discs. Hele and the guys at Meriden had done a great job!'

But it was Romero's Trident 750 that was fastest, averaging over 157mph (253km/h), followed by Hailwood Rocket III at 153mph (246km/h). The triples were so fast that Harley-Davidson protested them, and eventually the silencers had to be lengthened at the cost of some 200rpm. They were also reliable enough for the extra Tridents to be confirmed for Don Castro and factory tester Percy Tait to ride.

The 1970 Daytona 200 was controversial from the start. Talk had been of protests against the British early in the week, when it was obvious that the factory Triumphs and

Rocket III in a replica Rob North frame. This is modelled on the later 'lowboy' version with a lower headstock.

Another Rocket III in a Rob North-style frame, used for classic racing.

BSAs were using unhomologated five-speed gearboxes. But when Ralph Bryans crashed his Honda CR750 and everybody could see the four's unhomologated magnesium engine cases burning in the flames, all threats to protest illegal gearboxes evaporated. In the end the US importers had the required five-speed Quaife gearboxes on the shelf as an option to prevent any subsequent protests, but as Cook Neilson once told me, this was an era when you could have entered an AMA 'production' class on a stock Japanese 400, cruised around in dead last place, and then protested yourself to the win. Everybody cheated, so nobody protested.

But the notorious overheating of the triple's centre cylinder did for the Beezumphs. Hailwood's centre piston was the first to go, flipping his early lead into a DNF (did not finish), while Nixon's Trident did likewise with three laps to go when holding a fine lead over Dick Mann's Honda.

Romero took up the mantle, stalking Mann's sick Honda and coming within two seconds of winning; he did go on to win the AMA Grand National Championship for Triumph that year. The third place went to Castro on another Trident. It was a great result, Daytona being a race of attrition that almost did for the 10,000rpm Honda, never mind the 8,500rpm triples. But it was a turning point, and is rightly felt by some to be the most important motorcycle race in history. After Honda's win Harley-Davidson started to withdraw from road racing and focus on the juggernaut cruisers they are now famous for.

The British had thrown everything that money could buy at winning the race, and had still been beaten by a newcomer to big-bore motorcycling and the associated production-based racing. But the result was good enough to cement the British triples' reputation as the fastest motorcycle anyone could buy and, thanks to the US dealers, the versions delivered to customers were as reliable as any British motorcycle could be.

This hard work was rewarded with highly favourable press coverage, notably from *Cycle* magazine under Cook Neilson and Phil Schilling's tutelage. From a standing start – the most important metric to American stop light racers – the triple 'came out of the hole like a freight train', according to Neilson. The only criticism involved footrests that touched down too early, and a feeble front brake: oh, for the discs that BSA had rejected.

But as BSA sales manager Don Brown told Lindsay Brooke and David Gaylin in their book *Triumph Motorcycles in America*, 'the four just knocked the pins out from under us'. So back in England, plans were drawn up to try and correct that with a return to the Daytona 200.

BSA knew that defending their (and especially Triumph's) reputation in the critical US market was no longer a question of pride, but of survival. The decision to return to Daytona in 1971 and spend on a magnificent scale, with a five-rider dream team, was made on the promise of loans and money they simply did not have. And the dream almost came true, despite Paul Smart and Hailwood (again!) dropping out with centre-cylinder meltdowns. Dick Mann (curiously 'let go' by Honda) took a magnificent win for BSA, its first Daytona victory since Bobby Hill's win in 1954. Mann was followed home by Romero on his Triumph, followed by Don Emde on another BSA, to make the 1971 Daytona 200 a British one, two, three.

BSA might have been the parent company, and once the largest and most profitable motorcycle manufacturer on earth, but in truth Triumph was the more valuable name in the US, and the Daytona winners were really Triumphs. The design and development was Doug Hele's work from his Meriden office, and the engines were prepared at Meriden. Road racing had always meant America to the group, and it was Triumph people both in the UK and in the US who had worked to get these results. It was the same when the triples went trophy hunting at Bonneville Speed Week: the Triumph-powered bikes came away with the records.

After decades of ill will, the Triumph and BSA teams were increasingly focused on beating each other rather than the Japanese, in the US especially where there had been a shotgun marriage between the distributors and dealers. Meanwhile Honda, soon followed by their countrymen, focused on the product and dealer network. Honda cared not that BSA ridiculed their turn signals, electric starters and maintenance-free motorcycles (one British executive claiming that 'motorcyclists *like* to take their carburettors apart at the

An immaculately restored early Trident T150. Note the upright cylinders compared to the BSA triples.

weekend') because that was what Honda's team were told their prospective customers wanted.

Instead British management and workers focused on beating one another on the race tracks, patently forgetting they went 'racing on a Sunday to sell on Monday'. Because when BSA and Triumph won at Daytona there were no triples with US dealers, a mistake Honda would never have made.

Nonetheless the triples were developed into the most successful race bikes of their time, dominating the 750cc races in Europe and the US. Even Hopwood admitted the success was due to Hele's 'brilliance', and greatly criticised the BSA-Triumph board's reluctance to promote him from the drawing board. Hele was offered the chance to return to Norton with their then-new F750 team for 1972, but decided to stay with Triumph, moving to BSA's experimental team at Kitts Green. When BSA finally folded Hele turned down a job with the Japanese and joined outboard motor makers British Seagull in Dorset. Even in his seventies he was working as a freelancer on the Norton rotary.

While the triples greatest successes might have been due to the Triumph crew, notably with Slippery Sam, there is one BSA Rocket III legend that will live forever: Mallory Park's 1971 Race of the Year. Pat Slinn was there and is happy to tell the story in his own words.

> *8 August 1971 was a day I felt so proud to be an employee of BSA motorcycles, watching a BSA road bike beat what was undoubtedly one of the world's finest grand prix motorcycles ridden by one of the finest GP racers in the world. The MV Agusta 500 and Giacomo Agostini would prove no match for the BSA Rocket Three, albeit a specially built racing version ridden by John Cooper, one of the UK's finest short-circuit scratchers. Even after all these years, and many, many races later, that Race of the Year still stands out as one of the most exciting motorcycle races I have ever watched.*
>
> *For a week or so before the event I had been working in West Germany at the BSA/Triumph importers in Landsthul, down in the Rhine Phaltz. Landsthul was a pleasant town nestling close to a top-secret US air-force base at Ramstien and the huge US army base in Kaiserslautern. BSA and Triumph sold an awful lot of their products to the US troops in that part of Germany and, of course, 'just occasionally' they would go wrong! The financial problems at BSA/Triumph meant that their importers were not being paid for warranty work, so they had simply stopped doing any. In short, things were a mess, and I was the one running backwards and forwards between the UK and Germany to sort things out.*
>
> *So I was looking forward to the Race of the Year, booking my Saturday morning flight from Frankfurt back to Birmingham in plenty of time. Whenever I was in the UK I always visited the race shop at Meriden, so on my last trip I'd arranged to collect a pass for the event.*
>
> *Arriving at Mallory Park the first thing that I saw was an MV Agusta mechanic on his knees looking under the engine of John Cooper's BSA. Walking across I could see a group of very bemused BSA and Triumph mechanics muttering between themselves and wondering what on earth he was looking at.*
>
> *I can't really remember what type of lap times Cooper or Agostini managed during the practice sessions, although I can recall with clarity the distinctive wail of the MV's exhausts versus the BSA's bellowing as they powered out of Devil's Elbow and down the pit straight towards Gerard's. Doug Hele, the BSA/Triumph development engineer, stood nonchalantly at the side of the track and studied his stop watch – correction, two stop watches – one for Cooper, and one for Agostini. I don't think Doug believed a win was possible, and from memory the official practice times coming over the PA system certainly favoured Agostini and the MV.*
>
> *Shortly before Cooper and Agostini left the paddock for the race I spotted them speaking to each other and patting one another's arms, a gesture of mutual respect. John rode out and on to the start line, stopping just behind works BSA mechanic Steve Brown. Agostini lined up next to a pair of Italian mechanics. Courtesy of Doug Hele, my pass allowed me on to the starting grid to join the twenty or so highly tuned racing machines with mechanics warming their engines, all the while keeping expert eyes open for any last-minute problems.*
>
> *Standing amongst them had me thinking how vibrant and exciting the British motor-cycle racing scene was, and how I would like to be a part of it! Shortly before the start of the race I left the grid and walked up to the inside of the notorious Devil's Elbow,*

standing on the dirt bank at the same spot I would choose seven years later to watch my friend, the late, great Mike Hailwood (racing a bike that I would help prepare) win the British FI championship round on his Sports Motorcycles Ducati.

But back in 1971 I stood with Peter Howdle and Norrie White from Motor Cycle News, *together with (I think) John Brown from* The Motor Cycle, *the three of them legendary GP reporters. Norrie at least was backing Agostini to win. When the starter's flag dropped and the leading group raced towards Gerard's for the first time you could hear the howling MV above the BSA and Triumph triples as the first gaggle of riders peeled into the Elbow. Although I forget who was leading, Coop and Ago were definitely up at the front end of things. My abiding memory of the race will always be the wonderful sounds the MV and triples were making, and how you could almost hear them across the entire circuit, even when they were out of sight.*

Towards the end of the race Coop was making up the ground that he had lost to the MV, and when he briefly got a wheel in front of Ago the roar from the crowd almost drowned out the wailing exhausts. Starting the final lap Ago was still holding a small lead, but as they approached the hairpin there was cheering from spectators who could see the pair, and Peter Howdle shouted, 'He's through! He's going to do it!'

Clamouring to see who was going to emerge first from the hairpin I was elated to see Cooper in the lead! He was going to win! Even today I still feel the pride of being employed by BSA on the day of that remarkable victory. A BSA road-bike engine (even if breathed on by one of history's great motorcycle engineers) had beaten the most successful GP teaming in the world. The 100,000 crowd went wild: you couldn't see a single blade of grass on the bank opposite the pit area with people straining to get a look at Cooper and his equally amazing motorcycle.

I walked back to the BSA paddock, pushing myself between hundreds of people to congratulate John. He looked absolutely washed out, as he had all every right to be! A quick peek at his bike showed that it was clean, without any oil leaks. However, I was also aware that in a very short time I had an aeroplane to catch back home to Germany. Mrs Hele found me a nice hot 'cuppa' before I jumped into the car and headed off to beat the traffic jams. A few hours later I was back at in Germany having a late evening meal with my wife, Elaine.

The next day I had some small posters printed advertising BSA's win in the prestigious British Race of the Year, and hung them in the showroom windows of our three local dealers. Despite BSA and Triumph both struggling for sales, it was three days before the West German importers heard any official news of BSA's great victory. Apparently BSA's 'publicity' department wanted to wait for formal conformation of the result before they tried to gain any publicity for a truly remarkable achievement.

That it was no fluke was confirmed a week later, at Brands Hatch, when John 'Mooneyes' Cooper again beat Ago and the MV. Later in the year the Rocket III and Mooneyes won a 250-mile (400km) race in Ontario, but to no avail: BSA was a busted flush and, although the triple would live on, it would be as a Triumph Trident. 1971 had seen a revised Rocket III with its own 'beauty kit', looking as it should have done from the start, for the US market especially. It even staggered on into 1972 with the five-speed gearbox, again as it should have done from the start. And then it was gone.

THE BSA TRIPLE THAT NEVER WAS

Surely every motorcycle fan is familiar with the X75 Triumph Hurricane, the fabulous pseudo chopper designed by Craig Vetter of Windjammer fairing fame. Although apparently horrible to ride on its original extended forks and ribbed front tyre – to the extent that some were changed under warranty – it has become the most prized of the production triples, and reputedly the first classic Triumph bought by John Bloor. But it was a BSA project and, but for the same bickering the race teams invoked, would have been sold as a BSA.

In 1968 BSA's US vice president, Don Brown, had thought a halo model would boost sales and profile ahead of the Japanese launching their own heavyweights into the big bike market. He became convinced that such a motorcycle was essential once he'd seen the Ogle-styled triples, and realized

An X75 Hurricane, the Rocket III heritage obvious from the inclined cylinders.

that he would have to work in secret if BSA's main board really thought Ogle's work was the future. But he also realized this proved BSA would be open to new styling, where the Triumph fans from board level down to dealers and riders wanted the traditional Bonneville look.

Put in touch with Craig Vetter, who had shown a restyled Suzuki T500 that turned heads, Brown paid Vetter in cash and dealt with him so secretly that once he'd left BSA Vetter had to go back and ask the main board for his back pay – a total of $1,200 to style a motorcycle that would retail at $2,100. Sadly it was this sky-high price that led to the X75 collecting dust in US showrooms.

Vetter's prototype – with BSA badging – went to Umberslade Hall to be prepared for production. The first handbuilt models were shown to American dealers in early 1972, still with BSA writ large on the tank. But by the time the first models were delivered in June 1972 they were Triumphs, just as all the scarlet racing Rocket 3s had been repainted blue and had Triumph stickers applied. All that was left for BSA now was the lingering death that was the Ariel 3, a comedy moped that had nothing at all in common with the Rocket 3 beyond that final number.

A75 ROCKET III

Year: 1969
Displacement: 740cc
Bore/stroke: 67 x 70mm
Compression ratio: 9.5:1
Engine type: Four-stroke overhead-valve triple
Carburation: Three 26mm Amal Concentrics
Ignition system: Coil
Claimed power: 58bhp at 7,500rpm
Transmission: Single plate dry, four-speed unit-construction gearbox. Primary and final drive by chain
Brakes: Twin/single leading shoe drum front/rear
Wheels: 19in front and rear
Chassis: Telescopic front forks, twin shock absorber rear swinging arm, duplex frame
Weight: 498lb/226kg
Top speed: 115mph/185km/h

CHAPTER THIRTEEN

FIDDLING WHILE ROME BURNS

There are plenty of armchair management consultants who are of the opinion that the death of the British motorcycle industry was inevitable from the point at which it started to ignore the commuters and middleweight riders, who represent the future buyers of heavyweight motorcycles. Indeed Sir Bernard Docker had been lobbying, notably via the *Financial Times*, for shareholders and government tax collectors to rein in their expectations if BSA was to have enough cash to invest in new models and factories from the mid-fifties onwards. He was probably right, but as to taking on even the Japanese 250-350 class, he was already too late. The history of BSA – and, more intriguingly, of erstwhile survivors Harley-Davidson – is where fans of Western lightweights that might avoid sector retreat from the Japanese – and later others from Asia – are proved wrong.

Harley-Davidson spent the late sixties and much of the 1970s trying to keep to the accepted wisdom of fighting the Japanese motorcycle industry at all levels. Then owned by the AMF conglomerate, Harley bought up Aermacchi, developed a range of affordable two-stroke motorcycles from 125 to 350cc, and promoted them by winning 250 and 350 road-racing world championships. In the US they developed road racers based upon their iconic V-twins, notably Lucifer's Hammer, and campaigned endlessly to make sure their

A modified BSA single, Miss Behavin'. Too many at BSA were sadly doing the same, believing they could take on the Japanese motorcycle factories.

motorcycles had every chance to sell well and win races. But despite successful government and AMA lobbying (unlike the far less dynamic British motorcycle industry), Harley continued to lose money by building motorcycles that were overpriced for what they offered, and underprepared for what 1970s buyers expected of a brand new machine.

In despair AMF sold the company in 1981 to a team led by Vaughn Beals and Willie G. Davidson for $80 million. Beals was from a commercial diesel engine and logging machinery background, although Davidson was Harley-Davidson royalty. The team threw away the received wisdom, which they realized was based upon building motorcycles in the sort of numbers they would never be able to do. Instead they did what they did well – making sure that money was never wasted, including copying Japanese production techniques such as the 'just in time' delivery model. More cash was spent making sure the bikes were properly screwed together, making for happy customers and minimal warranty claims.

I once asked Gerald Davison, having seen Honda become a global colossus, if he'd thought the British motorcycle industry could have been saved. He didn't hesitate: 'Oh yes, of course. Go niche, but do it quickly. By the time Honda had arrived in the UK they were already the biggest factory in the world. The British were never going to beat them. But there would still be a market for sectors that the Japanese would never find profitable.'

Exhibit A would be Gerald's own Honda GB500, a short-lived model that used a big single from a trail bike in a retro-styled reimagining of a British bike. Another would be Ducati's best-selling model of the 1970s, the 900SS. A Rocket III motor in a Rob North frame would have been a worthy competitor. And the BSA/Triumph Hurricane XR75, with decent handling and brakes, would have been a far better motorcycle than any Harley-Davidson, let alone the Japanese 'custom' models that mimicked the look by the late seventies. Instead the British decided to take the Japanese head on, targeting the best-selling Honda 350.

TRIUMPH BANDIT/ BSA FURY 350

Edward Turner started his final motorcycle design at Triumph in 1968, the 350 Triumph Bandit and BSA Fury (prototyped as the Tiger 90 and Apollo respectively) promised for 1972.The four-stroke twin was fed by twin 27mm Amal carburettors and claimed 34bhp at 9,000rpm. With a weight of 345lb (157kg) and five-speed gearbox, the prototype was

Advertisement for the BSA/Triumph 350 twin that never made it to the showrooms. The chain-drive cover to the twin cams is evident in this view of the Triumph Bandit version.

The BSA Fury 350SS (street scrambler) version of the Hopwood/ Hele twin.

Offside view of the new three-fifty—this time BSA's "street scrambler" version, the Fury 350SS, differing from the "road" model only in the matter of exhaust layout. We regret that colour printing is denied us, to show the Fury's Plum Crazy colour scheme, "a course-flecked metallic purple . . ."

said to easily exceed 104mph (167km/h), and some claimed rather more.

Naturally Hopwood and Hele looked to fine tune the motor, but it quickly turned into a wholesale redesign as the pair took issue with many of Turner's ideas. The 360-degree crankshaft was traditional for British twins, but Hopwood and Hele redesigned the crankshaft to have a 180-degree throw. This mimicked the Honda twins and created less stress in a motor, although the design requires two carburettors. Cylinder head and valve designs were also reworked, as was the crankshaft, with the camchain moved from between the cylinders to the timing side of the engine.

Why a 350 when it would cost almost as much as a 750 twin to build? US dealers wanted a 350 twin to compete with Honda's, not knowing the Kawasaki 400 would shortly usurp it.

Turner imagined his 350 twin with a single downtube frame, but this was also discarded in favour of a double cradle item designed by Rob North. In essence Hopwood and Hele had started from scratch, and in the summer of 1970 their pre-production examples were given to magazines to test. The results were positive enough, but hardly the ringing endorsements that BSA and Triumph needed. *Cycle Guide* asserted their Bandit was 'probably the newest and freshest thing to come out of England in twenty years'. And yet it still had vertically split crankcases, despite being an all-new design. At least it didn't leak oil, and the magazine expected it to be priced competitively:

> *For a motorcycle that will sell in the area of $900, it is a lot of machine for the money. It's got a lot of performance, although we were unable to get any acceleration or top speed figures due to the nature of the weather and locale. One thing I can tell you, though, is that the motorcycle will run at 90mph all day long. The engine starts to pull strong at 3,000 to 3,500, and at nine grand it's still pulling.*

But *Motorcycle Sport Quarterly* noted that their Fury 'off the boil… lacked the lugging power of its popular Japanese contemporary'. They meant the Honda 350, of course, then on sale at $800. That $900 pricing suggestion for the British bikes was based upon American dealers' expectations. But when BSA's accountants had looked at the reality of building the bike, the Americans were asked how many 350s they might sell at between $1,500 and $1,600. And then warned that the electric starter would be an optional extra. And as noted, at the scale the British motorcycle industry was operating, a 350 twin would cost pretty much the same to build as a 750. BSA had learned the hard – and expensive – way, that they had missed their chance to take the Japanese head on.

So sadly, the 350 was not to be. Despite millions of pounds of investment, right down to printing marketing brochures and posters for dealers' walls and windows during the spring of 1972, the production costs were prohibitive. The viability of the entire BSA empire was now in question and in the public domain, leading to an announcement in November 1971 that the Fury and Bandit were 'on hold'. The only new model for 1972 would be the Ariel 3.

THE ARIEL 3 AND OTHER ANIMALS

The reason the Ariel 3 gets several paragraphs here, when the Sunbeam scooters only appear in the appendix of models built, and other BSA-branded ultra lightweights just get a brief footnote, is simply because the Ariel 3 is the bike that broke BSA. Its predecessors did not.

Down the years BSA had occasionally realized that the Bantam cash cow couldn't go on forever, and sometimes looked at the best-selling Italian 'hairdryers' – scooters with fan-cooled two-stroke motors – and thought that they could do better. So for the 1955 Earls Court Show, BSA offered a 198cc four-stroke scooter and the 70cc two-stroke Dandy (arguably BSA's second in-house stroker design), despite neither models having had any development. But despite being promised for spring the following year, both were quietly forgotten, although the Dandy did briefly go into production from 1957.

BSA didn't take this defeat lying down. The Italians had been selling their lightweight motorcycles in Britain for

An Ariel 3, a multi-million pound failure. Together with the investment in the 350 twin, BSA and their bankers could take no more punishment in the marketplace.
STEVE GLOVER

several years, and Honda had proven the demand for small capacity four-strokes in the US. BSA decided that the D1 Bantam should be dropped and a smaller, cheaper motorcycle would replace it. Val Page was already working on an ohc 50cc miniature Ariel Arrow when Edward Turner, then head of the BSA group, sketched out an ohv design and decreed it would be sold as an Ariel Pixie moped (42 x 38.9mm bore/stroke), while a big brother BSA Beagle and Starlight would be bored out to 47.6mm for a total of 70cc. Both had a pressed steel frame with a motorcycle's layout, rather than a scooter's.

Dealers were horrified, and had to be bullied into taking them. Buyers were horrified, especially when compared to the indestructible Honda Cub, but couldn't be bullied. These models, like the Dandy, drifted into oblivion. BSA management should have been chastised, should have listened to dealers and riders, and developed the big twins. Perhaps they might have decided there was a place for the occasional meaty big single.

After all, the 1981 team that rescued Harley had very few motorcyclists among their number, so they appreciated that this weakness meant listening to dealers and riders: this had long been the key to Triumph's success in the US. Willie G. Davidson spent his life visiting rallies and biker hotspots making notes, and talking to the people who had paid cold hard cash for their rides. Miguel Galluzzi, the man who designed the bike that saved Ducati, the Monster, did exactly the same. Only then did Galluzzi and Davidson approach their drawing boards and try sketching the next big thing. Doug Hele, incidentally, was famous among racers for sitting quietly while they spoke, all the while making copious notes.

Many of BSA's leaders were the antithesis of this. Harry Sturgeon had been one of the good guys, understanding the need to build bikes people would buy alongside the need to make a profit. This made him respected – but sadly he died of a brain tumour. His replacement in 1966 was the despised Lionel Jofeh, brought in from the aircraft industry, and in the eyes of many the one responsible for the end of BSA.

Jofeh had a reputation for removing anybody who disagreed with him from his inner circle; inevitably his inner circle did likewise, until the sky-high frame and Ogle styling became inevitable. Anybody who pointed out that the 1971 BSA 650 restyle just made it even more obvious that the 'power egg' motor – what the Americans called 'watermelons' – was from another era would have been gone by lunchtime. That only Triumph was profitable in BSA's motorcycle portfolio held no sway: despite the numbers proving their 650 twin was the main contributor to the bottom line, and dealers clamouring for a 750 twin rather than the heavyweight triple, made not a jot of difference. For BSA top brass, led by Jofeh – seemingly addicted to debt after spending over a million dollars racing at Daytona – stage two of the rescue plan was the Ariel 3.

THREE WHEELS ON MY WAGON

In 1967 George Wallis came up with a three-wheeled design for a moped that pivoted in the middle. His reckoning was that, by keeping the two back wheels upright, the bike remained stable at all times while the leaning front wheel kept the vehicle as manoeuvrable and as quick around corners as any two-wheeler. BSA fell for it and, thinking that the moped market would be its saviour, bought manufacturing rights. Wallis was appointed consultant, and BSA geared up to produce the Ariel 3, citing 'powerful market research' for their predicted lifeline. The Small Heath factory tooled up to build 2,000 units a week at a reputed cost of £2 million.

Wallis designed and built prototype trikes, some based on the Triumph Tina scooter with its automatic transmission driving the rear wheels via a differential. But according to the Wallis design company, 'the Ariel was designed by BSA design staff, who would not take any advice or suggestions on the design.'

In early summer 1970 the Ariel 3 was officially launched, priced at £100. That was about the same as a Vespa 90, and pricey for a 50cc moped when the average weekly wage was £32. Despite a flurry of publicity stunts the Ariel 3 failed to catch on, and instead became the swan song of the once great BSA group. Hundreds rather than the predicted thousands were sold, listed for three years, but all may as well have been built in 1970 and stockpiled.

The bizarre strapline for the Ariel 3 was 'Here it is, whatever it is'. Two BSA apprentices – Robert Tillotson and Patrick Tomkinson (son of endurance racer Mike Tomkinson) – made a trip to Barcelona for the 1970 Montjuic Park 24 Horas on a brace of the Ariels, making a 2,000-mile (3,200km) round trip carrying all their camping kit aboard the trikes. BSA accessories' subsidiary Motoplas offered goodies including a tinted windscreen and a very seventies 'Ariel 3' logo for the sides of the luggage compartments.

Japan's take on the Ariel 3, the Honda Gyro.
M. LOUIS

The late fifties Dandy 70 might have warned BSA off the ultra-lightweight and moped market. Checking the points necessitated removing the engine.

Tragically the 'powerful research' was wrong, and in 1971 BSA, trading with a £3 million loss, admitted to shareholders that 'errors of management contributed to the financial situation', glossing over the Ariel 3 debacle. The rights of the bike reverted to designer Wallis, who sold the idea to Honda as the Gyro. Gerald Davison at Honda UK remembers the Ariel 3, perhaps too well:

> *We had to crate up every new model and send it out to Honda in Japan. We were laughing as we packed up the little Ariel, saying 'what on earth are they going to make of this?' And of course they built it showing that you just need to know your market. In Japan there are people on street corners selling noodles from the back of mopeds. The Gyro meant that they didn't spill them as they rode along.*

But there wasn't anybody selling noodles on Britain's street corners.

BSA announced that redundancies would be needed. At a mass meeting the majority agreed to switch Small Heath's some 3,500 staff to short-time, to give up their annual bonus and to be more flexible. This led to fewer job losses, but it wasn't enough when BSA admitted to a debt pile of £22 million. The numbers were bad to start with, and got worse, and by 1972 BSA was effectively out of business. There was still hope, however, and with government aid something might have been rescued from the British motorcycle industry's very own car crash. Some have pointed to BSA's non-motorcycling interests being sold off at fire sale prices, but in 1973 the *Financial Times* thought otherwise:

> *No doubt BSA shareholders will cling to any straw offered them. For Manganese Bronze's part the deal looks a good one and on more favourable terms, presumably following the run on BSA's shares. Yet these are early days and Lord Shawcross' remark 'that more finance will be needed from some source to ensure the viability of the NVT [Norton Villiers Triumph] operation, of which I will be vice chairman', casts doubt about the eventual outcome.*

Or, as UK observer Jim Greening put it: 'Fresh faces just put old words and promises into new mouths.' The end was nigh.

LONG SLOW DEATHS – AND TRIUMPH ABANDONS SHIP

From Hopwood's arrival at Triumph in 1961 it seemed the Meriden factory was the favourite son. He and Hele hunkered down there, seemingly immune to the nonsense going on at Umberslade. They seemed not only autonomous but still hoping that their great ambitions might be fulfilled. The realization that they would not probably first dawned when US dealers' requests were turned down even by Turner, and the final straw must have been the prototype Trident in Bonneville swaddling clothes being handed to Ogle Design. BSA no longer seemed the parent company, but a wicked stepmother.

Industrial relations were always worse at Meriden than Small Heath, and the sit-in that followed BSA's collapse should not perhaps have come as a surprise. The BSA team went quietly into the night, having had their moments. Triumph survived, if only temporarily. A 750 T140 with A70 conrods came in July 1973, and a new conglomerate, Norton Villiers Triumph (NVT) soldiered on until February 1976 when the last Triumph Tridents were built for the government of Saudi Arabia.

There were also attempts to produce new models from existing parts – NVT built a few prototype P92s, a B50 engine in a BSA Fury/Triumph Bandit frame using Isolastic mountings from the Commando. There were also Triumph twins in BSA frames – but in truth these were just putting off the inevitable, although every payday that passed for people working at NVT was welcome. The Meriden co-operative achieved far more than anyone could have expected and built some fine motorcycles, but saddled with debt and little scope for development, was gone barely a decade after BSA fell.

REVIVALS PAST AND PRESENT

After the demise of BSA, Alan Clews bought up remaining B50 part stocks and set up Clews Competition Motorcycles (CCM), producing successful motocross bikes based on the B50. It survives today, notably with the Spitfire powered by a Husqvarna 600cc single-cylinder engine.

Dennis Poore bought the BSA naming rights in 1979 following the liquidation of NVT in 1978, under the 'BSA Company' banner, and hung very modest two-stroke singles on

The Yamaha-powered Tracker was another failed attempt to revive BSA.

BELOW: **The Tracker was supposed to offer an alternative to the Japanese, except it looked like a poor relation, with a small dealer network and a high price.**

DATA	125/6	175/6
Engine Type	Air cooled 2 str torque induction	Air cooled 2 str torque induction
Capacity	123cc	171cc
Bore and stroke	56/50mm	66/50mm
Comp ratio	7.2 : 1	6.8 : 1
Fuel	2 star	2 star
Lubrication	Autolube	Autolube
Transmission	Six-speed	Six-speed
Gear box/rear wheel sprocket	15T/49T	15T/49T
Rear chain	$\frac{1}{2}$" × $\frac{3}{16}$"	$\frac{1}{2}$" × $\frac{3}{16}$"
Electrical		
Ignition type	Flywheel magneto	C.D.I.
Battery	6v 4 amp-hour	6v 4 amp-hour
Headlamp	25/25watt	25/25watt
Tail/Stop Lamp	5/21 watt	5/21 watt
Tyres		
Front	2.75" × 21"	2.75" × 21"
Rear	3.50" × 18" Trials type	3.50" × 18" Trials type
Brakes		
Front	160mm drum	160mm drum
Rear	140mm drum	140mm drum
Capacities		
Fuel tank	1.0 gallons	1.2 gallons
Oil tank	1.7 pints	1.7 pints
Dimensions		
Dry weight	210 lbs (94kg)	210 lbs (94kg)
Overall length	78.7" (2000mm)	78.7" (2000mm)
Overall width	35" (899mm)	35" (899mm)
Overall height	45.1" (1145mm)	45.1" (1145mm)
Wheel base	52.5" (1320mm)	52.5" (1320mm)
Seat height	29.5" (750mm)	29.5" (750mm)
Ground clearance	9.5" (240mm)	9.5" (240mm)
Front fork travel	5.1" (130mm)	5.1" (130mm)
Rear wheel travel	4.9" (115mm)	4.9" (115mm)
Colour Choice	Red, Blue, White	Red, Blue, White

to the brand. Moving the company to Coventry, this much smaller concern produced basic Yamahaesque monoshock lightweights, including the sports moped Beaver and the trailie Brigand, with 50cc Franco Morini (not to be confused with Moto Morini) motors. The 125 and 175cc Tracker off-roader had Yamaha power. All were gone by 1981.

Yamaha power was wheeled out one more time for the BSA name in 1991, when the BSA Company merged with Mike Jackson's Norton International to form the new BSA Group. This was, in turn, taken over in 1997 to become BSA Regal, based in Southampton, and still carries on as a non-motorcycle business. A small batch of retro-styled café racers followed, the Yamaha SR400-powered 'BSA Gold SR'. These were built primarily for export to Japan. Since then, despite various suggestions including electric machines, little has been built, although there was a short-lived clothing brand and a prototype Bantam designed by Brits Seymour Powell, which MZ pondered in their 1990s Rotax period.

And then, in October 2016, the giant Indian Mahindra Group, which also owns Peugeot motorcycles and the rights to the Jawa name, bought all BSA rights, bar the gun and sight business that still lives in Armoury Road.

BSA-MAHINDRA

Indian tractor giant Mahindra bought the rights to the BSA name with plans to start building motorcycles for export, starting in 2019 – although at the time of writing, late 2019 – nothing more has been announced. Mahindra is not only the world's largest producer of tractors, they have also been producing cheap, lightweight two-stroke commuter bikes that are sold across Asia. Then they acquired 51 per cent of Peugeot Scooters before buying the Jawa brand. The stated aim is to build BSAs in their factory complex in Pithampur, Madhya Predesh, from 2019 to sell in Europe and the US: Royal Enfield is surely an inspiration.

But it has been the Jawa on which Mahindra focused, probably because those 300cc four-stroke singles have been massive sellers closer to home. The demand for the Jawa, far outstripping supply, alongside the issues of developing and building a motorcycle that will be of a quality, reliability and performance acceptable to the US and European markets, will likely delay the launch of these new BSAs: after all, Royal Enfield delayed the UK launch of the Interceptor and Himalaya by a year to make sure that teething problems were dealt with away from the eyes of picky Westerners.

ANY ANSWERS?

So, having answered the question 'where did it all go?', with the benefit of hindsight could BSA motorcycles have survived? For the Triumph twins the answer is almost certainly yes. The failings of management largely came down to a lack of preparedness to listen and learn – surely a lesson for us all. Picking managers and board members for their MBA rather than their club memberships would have been a start, but the preparedness of those men to listen would have made far more difference. As we have learned from Stan Dibben and Pat Slinn, most managers and designers were old men thinking about their retirement rather than where the business might be in ten years' time. Dealers, especially in America, had been asking for 750cc twins with five-speed gearboxes since the 1950s: the British chose not to build them. The desire for electric starts and less vibration followed.

By the time these issues were addressed – notably with Norton's Isolastic vibration dampening that worked brilliantly on the Commando and P92 'BSA' single, as well as the prototype big bore Trident – it was too late. That Hopwood and Hele were still prototyping vertically split crankcases with the 350 Bandit and Fury was foolhardy at best, and that they imagined they could build such a motorcycle at a similar price to Honda suggested they should have been listening to accountants as well as dealers.

There was also a lack of acceptance, notably with Hopwood and Hele, that the BSA group's place in the world had changed. Chased from being the world's largest motorcycle manufacturer by Honda, swiftly followed by their fellow Japanese, the pair were still prototyping rotary engines, big bore Isolastic Tridents and the 4-cylinder Triumph Quadrant while dreaming of a 1000cc V5. The BSA group were never going to be able to offer such diversity, and certainly not at a price to match the Japanese.

And what did BSA and Triumph fans know of such engine layouts? Or indeed a management that was convinced by 'powerful market research' that the Ariel 3 would answer their prayers, while dealers across the world begged for a 750cc Bonneville with five speeds, an electric start, disc brakes and Jack Wilkes styling? If it didn't leak oil or vibrate, so much the better: balancer shafts or, more realistically,

Isolastic engine mounts would have solved the later problem in the short term at least.

But by the time the T140V that met most of these requirements was on sale – and selling apace – it was too late. Meriden's co-operative never had the resources to keep up with world market demands on emissions and noise levels. And nor had BSA, once they had thrown everything they and their bankers had at winning Daytona and a dohc 350 twin, never mind the Ariel 3.

From a distance it seems that misplaced pride killed the British motorcycle industry: the understandable post-war hubris that is still talked of in business schools across the world. But given the talent, commitment and extraordinary enthusiasm of most of the people involved, from the shop floor workers to the dealers, it might have been very different. If you still doubt that, do something none of the people I studied business alongside would do: go and ride a big BSA (or Triumph) twin that's been put together with love. They are still outstanding motorcycles that pass the test Enzo Ferrari applied to the cars he loved: you cannot walk away without looking back at them over your shoulder. So, while it is tragic that BSA collapsed, be thankful for the many fine motorcycles they left behind. I'll have a Rob North Rocket III, and Pat Slinn a Gold Star. Thank you, and goodnight.

Even at the end BSA were working on new products : this is Project 55 (PO55) a 4-valve-head engine tested at Umberslade Hall in 1970.

BSA was once held in high regard by many, and affection for the marque was justifiable.

BSA PRODUCTION MODELS YEAR BY YEAR

1912
3.5HP two-speed 500
4.25HP three-speed 1912 550

1914
3.5HP two-speed 500

1915
4.25HP three-speed 550
4.25HP chain-cum-belt three-speed 550

1916
4.25HP chain-cum-belt three-speed 550

1917
4.25HP chain-cum-belt three-speed 550

1918
4.25HP chain-cum-belt three-speed 550

1919
4.25HP chain-cum-belt three-speed 550

1920
4.25HP chain-cum-belt three-speed 550
6/7HP twin 770

1921
6/7HP twin 770

1922
4.5HP de Luxe 550
4.25HP H2 OR K2 550
6/7HP twin 770

1923
4.5HP de Luxe 550
4.25HP H2 OR K2 550
2.75HP 350
6/7HP twin 770
8HP twin 1000

1924
2.49HP Standard 250
4.5HP Light 550
3.5HP 350
2.75HP 350
4.98HP de Luxe 500
8HP Taxi 1000
8HP twin 1000
8HP twin Colonial 1000

1925
2.49HP Standard de Luxe 250
3.49HP 350
3.49HP 350
4.5HP Light 450
3.5HP 350
3.49HP ohv Super 350
4.98HP de Luxe 500
7.70HP de Luxe 750
7.70HP Light 750
9.86HP Colonial 1000
9.86HP de Luxe 1000
9.86HP Light 1000

1926
5.57HP Light 550
2.49 350

5.57HP de Luxe 550
4.93HP Standard 500
4.98HP de Luxe 500
4.98HP Standard 500
3.49HP ohv Super 350
7.70HP de Luxe 750
7.70HP Light 750
9.86HP Colonial 1000
9.86HP de Luxe 1000
9.86HP Light 1000

1927
7.70HP de Luxe 750
7.70HP Light 750
2.49HP Standard de Luxe 250
9.86HP de Luxe 1000
3.49HP ohv Super 350
5.57HP 550
4.93HP Standard & Special Sports 500
4.98HP de Luxe 500
4.93HP ohv 500

1928
7.70HP twin 750
2.49HP 250
9.86HP twin 1000
3.49HP ohv Super 350
3.49HP 350
5.57HP 550
3.49HP ohv Standard 350
4.93HP 500
4.93HP 500
1.74HP two stroke 150
4.93HP ohv 500

1929
7.70HP E29 750
2.49HP B29 de Luxe 250
7.70HP E29 de Luxe 750
9.86HP G29 World Tour 1000
3.49HP L29 ohv twin-port Sloper 350
3.49HP L29 de Luxe 350
5.57HP H29 de Luxe 550
4.93HP S29 twin-port Light 500
3.49HP L29 ohv 350
4.93HP S29 Standard 500
1.75HP A29 Standard two-stroke 150
4.93HP S29 ohv twin-port Sloper 500
4.93HP S29 de Luxe 500
4.93HP ohv Dirt Track 500
1.75HP Standard de Luxe two-stroke 150

1930
2.49HP B30-3 250
4.93HP S30-19 ohv Light 500
4.93HP S30-13 ohv de Luxe 500
2.49HP B30-4 ohv 250
4.93HP S30-7 500
4.93HP S30-9 de Luxe 500
3.49HP L30-5 350
3.49HP L30-6 Commercial 350
4.93HP S30-18 Light 500
3.49HP L30-11 ohv de Luxe 350
4.93HP S30-12 ohv 500
5.57HP H30-10 de Luxe 550
5.57HP H30-8 550
7.70HP E30-14 twin 750
9.86HP G30-15 twin 1000
9.86HP G30-16 twin World Tour 1000
1.74HP A30-2 3 speed two-stroke 150

1931
2.49HP B31-1 250
4.93HP S31-10 ohv de Luxe 500
7.70HP E31-11 twin 2gal tank 750
7.70HP E31-11 twin 3gal tank 750
9.86HP G31-12 twin World Tour 1000
2.49HP B31-2 ohv 250
2.49HP B31-3 ohv de Luxe 250
3.49HP L31-4 350
3.49HP L31-5 de Luxe 350
3.49HP L31-6 ohv de Luxe 350
4.93HP S31-7 500
5.57HP H31-8 de Luxe 550
4.93HP S31-9 ohv 500
2.49HP L31-5 Post Office 250

1932
2.49HP B32-1 ohv 250
9.86HP G32-10 1000
3.49HP L32-5 ohv Blue Star 350
4.99HP W32-7 ohv Blue Star 500

3.49HP L32-2 350
3.49HP L32-3 ohv 350
3.49HP L32-4 de Luxe 350
3.49HP L32-5 ohv Blue Star 350
3.49HP L32-5 ohv de Luxe 350
4.99HP W32-6 500
4.99HP W32-7 ohv Blue Star 500
4.99HP W32-7 ohv 500
4.99HP S32-8 ohv de Luxe 500
5.57HP H32-9 de Luxe 550

1933
2.49HP B33-1 250
5.95HP M33-10 600
5.95HP M33-11 ohv 600
9.86HP G33-12 twin Light 1000
9.86HP G33-13 twin World Tour 1000
9.98HP G33-14 twin War Office 1000
2.49HP B33-2 ohv S.P. 250
2.49HP B33-3 Blue Star Junior 250
3.48HP R33-4 ohv 350
3.48HP R33-5 ohv Blue Star 350
4.99HP W33-6 500
4.99HP W33-6 Post Office 500
4.99HP W33-7 ohv 500
4.99HP W33-8 ohv Blue Star 500
4.99HP W33-9 ohv 500

1934
2.49HP B34-1 250
4.99HP W34-10 ohv Special 500
4.98HP J34-11 ohv twin 500
5.95HP M34-12 600
5.95HP M34-13 ohv 600
9.86HP G34-14 twin World Tour 1000
1.49HP X34-0 ohv 150
2.49HP B34-17 ohv Sports 250
2.49HP B34-2 ohv 250
2.49HP B34-3 Blue Star Junior 250
3.48HP R34-4 ohv 350
3.48HP R34-5 ohv Blue Star 350
3.48HP R34-6 ohv Special 350
4.99HP W34-7 500
4.99HP W34-8 ohv 500
4.99HP W34-9 ohv Blue Star 500

1935
1.49HP X35-0 ohv 150
2.49HP B35-1 250
5.95HP M35-10 500
5.95HP M35-11 ohv 600
4.98HP J35-12 ohv twin 500
9.86HP G35-14 twin 1000
7.50HP J35-15 ohv Twin War Office 750
3.48HP R35-17 ohv twin-port 350
2.49HP B35-2 ohv 250
2.49HP B35-3 ohv de Luxe 250
3.48HP R35-4 ohv de Luxe 350
3.48HP R35-5 ohv Blue Star 350
4.98HP W35-6 500
4.99HP W35-7 ohv 500
4.99HP W35-8 ohv Blue Star 500
4.99HP W35-9 ohv Special 500

1936
3.48HP R5 ohv Empire Star 350
4.96HP Q8 ohv Empire Star 500
1.49HP X0 ohv 150
2.49HP B1 250
5.95HP M10 600
4.98HP J12 ohv twin 500
7.48HP Y13 ohv twin 750
9.86HP G14 twin D14 1000
3.48HP R17 ohv 350
2.49HP B18 ohv Light de Luxe 250
3.48HP R19 ohv Competition 350
2.49HP B2 ohv 250
3.48HP R20 ohv New Blue Star 350
4.96HP Q21 ohv New Blue Star 500
2.49HP B3 ohv de Luxe 250
3.48HP R4 ohv de Luxe 350
3.48HP R5 ohv Empire Star 350
4.99HP W6 500
4.96HP Q7 ohv 500
4.96HP Q8 ohv Empire Star 500

1937
B20 Tourer 250
B21 ohv Sports 250
B22 ohv Empire Star 250
B23 Tourer 350
B24 ohv Empire Star 350

B25 ohv Competition 350
B26 ohv Sports 350
G14 twin 1000
M19 ohv de Luxe 350
M20 Tourer 500
M21 Tourer 600
M22 ohv Sports 500
M23 ohv Empire Star 500
Y13 ohv twin 750

1938
B20 Tourer 250
B21 ohv Sports 250
B22 ohv Empire Star 250
B23 Tourer 350
B24 ohv Empire Star 350
B25 ohv Competition 350
B26 ohv Sports 350
C10 250
C11 250
G14 twin 1000
M19 ohv de Luxe 350
M20 Tourer 500
M21 Tourer 600
M22 ohv Sports 500
M23 ohv Empire Star 500
M24 Gold Star 500
Y13 ohv twin 750

1939
B21 de Luxe 250
B23 de Luxe 500
B24 Silver Star 500
B25 Competition 350
B26 350
C10 de Luxe 250
C11 250
G14 twin 1000
B21 Standard 250
B23 Standard 350
C10 Standard 250
M22 Standard 500
M20 de Luxe 500
M21 600
M23 Silver Star 500
M24 Gold Star 500
M20 Standard 500

1940
B29 Silver Sports 350
W.D.B30 350
C10 250
C11 250
C12 350
G14 twin 1000
W.D. M20 500
W.D. M20 500
W.D. M20 500
W.D. M20 500
W.D. M20 500
M20 500
M21 600
M23 Silver Star 500

1941
B30 350
C10 250
C11 250
C12 350
W.D. M20 500

1942–1944
W.D. M20 500

1945
B31 350
C10 250
C11 250
M20 500

1946
B31 350
B32 Competition 350
C10 250
C11 250
M20 500
M21 600

1947
A7 500
B31 350
B32 Competition 350

B33 500
B34 Competition 500
C10 250
C11 250
M20 500
M21 600

1948
A7 500
B31 350
B32 Competition 350
B33 500
B34 Competition 500
C10 250
C11 250
M20 500
M21 600
M33 500

1949
D1 Bantam 125
A7 500
A7S Star Twin 500
B31 350
B32 Competition 350
B32GS Gold Star 350
B33 500
B34 Competition 500
B34GS Gold Star 500
C10 250
C10 Australia 250
C11 250
M20 500
M21 600
M21 Batavia 600
M33 500

1950
D1 Bantam 125
D1 Bantam GPO 125
A10 Golden Flash 650
A7 500
A7S Star Twin 500
B31 350
B31 alloy motor 350
B32 Competition (now with alloy engine option) 350
B32GS Gold Star 350
B33 (now with alloy engine option) 500
B34 Competition (now with alloy engine option) 500
B34GS Gold Star 500
C10 250
C10 Australia 250
C11 250
M20 500
M21 600
M21 Dutch Automobile Association 600
M33 500

1951
A7 500
A7S Star Twin 500
D1 Bantam GPO 125
D1 Bantam 125
A10 Golden Flash 650
B31 350
B32 Competition 350
B32GS Gold Star 1951 350
B33 500
B34 Competition 500
B34GS Gold Star 500
C10 (now with four-speed option) 250
C10 Australia 250
C11 (now with four-speed option) 250
M20 500
M21 600
M33 500

1952
A7 500
A7S Star Twin 500
D1 Bantam 125
D1 Bantam GPO 125
A10 Golden Flash 650
B31 350
B32 Competition 350
B32GS Gold Star 350
B32 Gold Star Clubman's 350
B33 500
B34 Competition 500
B34 Competition (sand and die-cast engine options) 500
B34GS Gold Star (sand and die-cast engine options) 500
C10 250

C11 250
M20 500
M21 600
M33 500

1953

A10 Golden Flash 650
A10SF Super Flash 650
A7 500
A7ST Star Twin 500
B31 350
B32 Competition 350
B32 Competition 350
B32GS Gold Star 350
B33 500
B34 Competition 1953 500
B34GS Gold Star 500
C10 250
C10 (four-speed now standard) 250
C11 (including four-speed option) 250
D1 Bantam 125
D1 Bantam GPO 125
M20 500
M21 600
M33 500

1954

A10SF Super Flash 650
A7 500
A7ST Star Twin 500
B31 350
B32 Competition (alloy motor now standard) 350
B32GS Gold Star 350
B33 500
B34 Competition 500
B34GS Gold Star 500
B34GSD Gold Star Daytona 500
C10L 250
C11G 250
C11G (including four-speed option) 250
D1 Bantam Competition 125
D1 Bantam 125
D3 Bantam 150
D3 Bantam Competition 150
D1 Bantam GPO 125
M20 500
M21 600
M33 500
A10 Golden Flash 650
A10R Road Rocket 650
A10SF Super Flash 650
A7SS Shooting Star 500
B32GS Gold Star New Clubman's 350
B34GS Gold Star New Clubman's 500

1955

B31 350
B32 Competition 350
B32GS Gold Star 350
B33 500
B34 Competition 500
B34GS Gold Star 500
C10L 250
C11G (including four-speed option) 250
D3 Bantam 153
M20 500
M21 600
M33 500
A10R Road Rocket 650
A7 500
A7SS Shooting Star 500
A10 Golden Flash 650
B32GS Gold Star Clubman's 350
B34GS Gold Star Clubman's 500
B32GS Gold Star (swinging-arm frame option introduced) 350
D1 Bantam 125

1956

B31 350
B32 Competition Clipper 350
B33 500
B34 Competition Clipper 500
C10L 250
C11G (four-speed now standard) 250
C12 250
D3 Bantam 150
M21 600
M33 500
A10 Golden Flash 650
A10R Road Rocket 650
A7 500

A7SS Shooting Star 500
B32GS Gold Star 350
B34GS Gold Star 500
B34GS Gold Star USA 500
B34GS Gold Star (new cylinder head) 500
D1 Bantam 125
D1 Bantam GPO 125

1957
B31 350
B32 Competition 350
B33 1957 500
B34 Competition 500
C10L 250
C12 250
D3 Bantam 150
M20 500
M21 600
M33 500
A10 Golden Flash 650
A10R Road Rocket 650
A10S Spitfire Scrambler 650
A7 500
A7SS Shooting Star 500
B32GS Gold Star 350
B34GS Gold Star 500
B34GS Gold Star US 500
B34GS Gold Star (new cylinder head) 500
D1 Bantam 125
D1 Bantam GPO 125
Dandy 70

1958
C12 250
M21 600
A10R Super Rocket 650
A10S Spitfire Scrambler 650
A7 500
A7SS Shooting Star 500
A10 Golden Flash 650
B34GS Gold Star 500
D1 Bantam 125
D1 Bantam GPO 125
Dandy 70
D5 Bantam 175
B31 350
B33 500

1959
M21 600
C15 Star 250
C15 Scrambles 250
C15 Trials 250
A10R Super Rocket 650
A10S Spitfire Scrambler 650
A7 500
A7SS Shooting Star 500
A10 Golden Flash 650
B34GS Gold Star 350
B34GS Gold Star 500
B34GS Gold Star Catalina 500
D1 Bantam 125
D1 Bantam GPO 125
Dandy 70
D7 Bantam 175
B31 350
B33 500
B2/B2S Sunbeam scooter (S model with, otherwise without electric start) 250

1960
M21 600
C15 Star 250
C15 Scrambles 250
C15 Trials 250
A7 500
A7SS Shooting Star 500
A10 Golden Flash 650
A10R Super Rocket 650
A10S Spitfire Scrambler 650
B32GS Gold Star 350
B34GS Gold Star 500
B34GS Gold Star Catalina 500
D1 Bantam 125
D1 Bantam GPO 125
Dandy 70
D7 Bantam 175
B33 500
B1 Sunbeam scooter S 175
B2/B2S Sunbeam scooter 250

1961
B40 Star 350
M21 600
C15 Star 250
C15 Scrambles 250
C15 SS80 Sports Star 80 250
C15 Trials 250
A7 500
A7 Shooting Star 500
A10 Golden Flash 650
A10 Golden Flash 650
A10R Super Rocket 650
A10S Spitfire Scrambler 650
B32GS Gold Star 350
DB34GS Gold Star 500
DB34GS Gold Star Catalina 500
D1 Bantam 125
D1 Bantam GPO 1961 125
Dandy 70
D7 Bantam 175
B1 Sunbeam scooter 175
B2/B2S Sunbeam scooter 250

1962
A50 Star Twin 500
A65 Star Twin 650
B40 Star 350
B40 SS90 Sports Star 90 350
M21 600
C15 Star 250
C15 Scrambles 250
C15 Scrambles Special 250
C15 SS80 Sports Star 80 250
C15 Trials 250
C15 Trials Special 250
A7 500
A7SS Shooting Star 500
A10 Golden Flash 650
A10R Super Rocket 650
A10S Spitfire Scrambler 650
A10RGS Rocket Gold Star 650
B32GS Gold Star 350
B34GS Gold Star 500
B34GS Gold Star Catalina 500
D1 Bantam 125
D1 Bantam GPO 125
Dandy 70
D7 Bantam 175
B1/B1S Sunbeam scooter 175
B2/B2S Sunbeam scooter 250

1963
A50 Star Twin 500
A65 Star Twin 650
B40 Star 350
B40 Star USA 350
B40 SS90 Sports Star 90 350
M21 600
C15 Star 250
C15 Starfire Roadster 250
C15 Star America 250
C15 police 250
C15 Scrambles 250
C15 Starfire Roadster 250
C15 SS80 Sports Star 80 250
C15 Trials 250
C15 Trials Pastoral 250
A10 Golden Flash 650
A10R Super Rocket 650
A10S Spitfire Scrambler 650
A10RGS Rocket Gold Star 650
B34GS Gold Star 500
B34GS Gold Star Catalina 500
D1 Bantam 125
D7 Bantam 175
D7 Bantam Trail 175
D7 Bantam America 175
D7 Bantam police 175
B1 Sunbeam scooter 1963 S 12498 B 31825 175
B2/B2S Sunbeam scooter 250

1964
A50 Star 500
A50 police 500
A50C Cyclone 500
A65 Star 1964 650
A65 police 650
A65R Rocket 650
A65T Thunderbolt Rocket 650
A65R Rocket 650
A65L Lightning Rocket 650
A65SH Spitfire Hornet 650

B40 Star 350
B40 Super Star USA 350
B40 police 350
B40 SS90 Sports Star 90 350
B40 Enduro Star USA 350
C15 Star 250
C15 Star America 250
C15 police 250
C15 Scrambles 250
C15 Starfire Roadster 250
C15 SS80 Sports Star 80 250
C15 Trials Pastoral 250
C15 Trials 250
D1 Bantam 125
D7 Bantam 175
D7 Bantam Trial 175
D7 Bantam America 1964 175
Beagle 75
Starlite 75
B1 Sunbeam scooter 175

1965
A50 Star 500
A50 police 500
A50CC Cyclone Competition 500
A50C Cyclone road model 500
A50 Cyclone Competition UK 500
A50 Cyclone UK 500
A65 Star 650
A65 police 650
A65R Rocket 650
A65L Lightning Rocket 650
A65 Lightning 650
A65 Lightning Clubman's 650
A65SH Spitfire Hornet 650
B40 Star 350
B40 Sportsman USA 350
B40 Enduro Star USA 350
B40 police 350
B40 SS90 Sports Star 90 350
C15 Star 250
C15 Star America 250
C15 police 250
C15 Scrambles 250
C15 Starfire Roadster 250
C15 SS80 Sports Star 80 250
C15 Trials 250
C15 Trials Cat 250
C15 Trials Pastoral 250
D1 Bantam GPO 125
D7 Bantam 175
D7 Bantam Pastoral 175
D7 Bantam Trial Bronc 175
Beagle 75
Starlite 75
B1 Sunbeam scooter 175

1966
A50R Royal Star 500
A50W Wasp 500
A65H Hornet 650
A65L Lightning 1966 650
A65LC Lightning Clubman's 650
A65S Spitfire MKII 650
A65T Thunderbolt 650
B40 Star 350
B44 Victor Grand Prix 440
B44 Victor Enduro 441
C15 Star 250
C15 Sportsman 250
D7 Silver Bantam 175
D7 Bantam de Luxe 175
D7 Bantam Silver and de Luxe 175
D7 Bantam GPO 175

1967
A50R Royal Star 500
A50W Wasp 500
A65H Hornet 650
A65L Lightning 650
A65SA Spitfire MKIII 650
A65T Thunderbolt 650
B40 Star 350
B40 military Australia 350
B40 military 350
B44 Victor Grand Prix 441
B44 Victor Enduro 441
B44 Victor Roadster 441
C15 Star 250
C15 police 250
C15 Sportsman 250
B25 Starfire USA 250

C25 Barracuda 250
D10 Bantam three-/four-speed Silver 175
D10 Bantam GPO 175
D10 Bantam four-speed Supreme 175
D10 Bantam four-speed Sport 175
D10 Bushman 175
D10 Bushman Pastoral 175

1968
A50R Royal Star 500
A50W Wasp 500
A65F Firebird Scrambler 650
A65L Lightning 650
A65S Spitfire MKIV 650
A65T Thunderbolt 650
B25 Starfire 250
B25 Fleetstar 250
B40 military Denmark 350
B40 military 350
B44 Shooting Star 441
B44 Victor Special 441
D13 Bantam Supreme 175
D13 Bantam Sports 175
D13 Bantam Bushman 175
D14/4 Bantam 175
D14/4 Bantam Sports 175
D14/4 Bantam Bushman 175

1969
A50 Royal Star 500
A65F Firebird Scrambler 650
A65L Lightning 650
A65T Thunderbolt 650
A75 four-/five-speed Rocket III 750
B25FS Fleetstar 250
B25 Starfire 250
B40 military (army) 350
B40 military Denmark 350
B40 military (navy) 350
B40 military 1969 350
B44SS Shooting Star 441
B44VS Victor Special 441
B175 Bantam 175
B175 Bantam Bushman 175
B40 Roughrider 350

1970
A50 Royal Star 500
A65 Firebird Scrambler 650
A65 Lightning 650
A65 Thunderbolt 650
A75 Rocket III four-/five-speed 1970 750
B25FS Fleetstar 250
B25 Starfire 250
B40 military Denmark 350
B44 Shooting Star 441
B44 Victor Special 441
B175 Bantam 175
B175 Bantam Bushman 175

1971
A65 Firebird Scrambler 650
A65 Lightning 650
A65 Thunderbolt 650
A75 Rocket III four-/five-speed 750
B25FS Fleetstar 250
B25SS Gold Star 250
B25 Victor Trial 250
B50 Victor MX 500
B50SS Gold Star 500
B50 Victor Trial 500
B175 Bantam 175
E35R Fury 350
E35SS Fury SS 350

1972
A65 Lightning 650
A65 Thunderbolt 650
A70 Lightning 750
A75 Rocket III four-/five-speed 750
B50 Victor MX 500
B50SS Gold Star 500
B50 Victor Trial 500
Ariel 3

1973
B50 Victor MX 500
Ariel 3

1974
Ariel 3
T65 650

INDEX